Love and Resistance

POEMS

by Nizar Qabbani

Translated by Rana Bitar
With edits by Robert Bensen

Love and Resistance

©2025 by Rana Bitar

Fernwood Press
Newberg, Oregon
www.fernwoodpress.com

All rights reserved. No part may be reproduced
for any commercial purpose by any method without
permission in writing from the copyright holder.

Printed in the United States of America

Cover and page design: Mareesa Fawver Moss
Cover art: "A Village in the Sun" by Mahmoud Hammad, 1951,
  in the holdings of the National Museum in Damascus, Syria.

ISBN 978-1-59498-158-6

For Damascus—
Across time and distance, your Jasmines whisper in my ears, still.

Contents

About the Book 7
Introduction to Qabbani's World 11
Why I Write 36
Maritime Poem 40
I Love You to Lift Up the Sky 42
African Breasts 54
When I Love You 60
I Love You So Much 66
Your Body Is My Map 70
The Book of Love 74
I Love You and the Rest to Come 96
Squares 102
Painting with Words 108
The Trial 112
Standing in Lines 114
The Train of Sorrows 118
Bread, Hashish, and the Moon 120
A Lesson in Drawing 126
Balqis 132

Notes in the Book of Defeat 160
I Read Your Body, and I Educate Myself 174
Citizens Without a Nation 180

Biographies 191
Acknowledgments 195

About the Book

Nizar Qabbani (1923-1998) was one of the most influential poets in Syria and the Middle East. His massive popularity came from his skill in writing poetry using a conversational language that anyone could read, understand, and recite. He devoted his early writing to advocating freeing women from the strictures of traditional sexual and gender roles. Later, he broadened his purpose to expose the follies of Arab governments and the oppressive aspects of traditional lifeways. His early love poems captivated young women and men looking to challenge the existing taboos, and later, his political poems shook governmental establishments and regimes. Qabbani used common words to create uncommon ideas, and with the simplicity of his words, he spoke the unspoken and the prohibited. As a result, he was chased and threatened and spent most of his life living and writing outside Syria.

The book's introduction chronicles Mr. Qabbani's life and explains the background, the social climate, and the circumstances from which each stage of his poetry emerged. The introduction's quotations are excerpted from longer poems to give a glimpse of how his style and subjects changed in response to events in his love life and the political life of his people.

No extant translation of Mr. Qabbani's work comprehends the breadth and relation between his amatory and political verse. No translations present poems in their entirety, preferring to extract sound-bites that sentimentalize the passion and intellect in the originals.

We selected poems in *Love and Resistance* for their breadth of representation, their influence in the Arab world, and their poetic prowess. The first section includes eleven love poems; the second has nine political poems. The translated poems are supplemented with footnotes to explain words or names in their historical and cultural context.

Let me bring you from Damascus
a handful of jasmines
The white is whispers of love
and the scent is the ink of daring

Introduction to Qabbani's World

When Nizar Qabbani (1923-1998) published his first book of poetry in Damascus, Syria, in 1944, he started a revolution in the Arab world. Qabbani's collection of 28 poems titled *The Brunette Told Me* broke taboos and violated the deeply rooted behavioral and moral codes of that time. Qabbani's collection gave a voice to the Arab women—women who were not allowed then to speak to men except their husbands and sons and were expected to keep their faces veiled. The collection's mere title suggested that a woman was talking to the poet directly—a radical proposition in the Arab world at that time. For a poet to give women a voice to inspire his poems freely was unheard of and forbidden at that time in Syria. Qabbani self-published 300 copies of the book at his own expense while he was a student at law school. This collection of 28 poems, which he wrote between the ages of 16 and 22, managed to turn the Syrian people's attention from fighting the French colonizers to attacking him.

An Explosion of Love Poems

What was in this collection that was so explosive? Qabbani's poems were free expressions of love never written or articulated in the Arabic world before; they broke the taboos in subjects and the choice of words. Such poetic images had never been allowed to be seen or thought of outside the tightly closed doors of bedrooms. Love and sex were under the highest prohibition in the conservative religious Arab world, especially in Damascus. Open discourse on these subjects threatened Arabic values more than the subjugation to a foreign power and limited freedom. In that world, the pride of the pious derived from adhering to their moral values was much more crucial to their identity than the pride of their national sovereignty and human rights.

But Qabbani believed that seeking freedom should apply to everything; people cannot be free from a foreign invader without first expressing themselves without fear of persecution. He believed that a nation couldn't produce free citizens if those citizens couldn't allow themselves to think, feel, and speak freely. At that time in Syria, the chains of the foreign French invaders were as tight as those of social and religious conservatism. Qabbani clearly saw the connection, and he lived through and for his vision.

Qabbani insisted on writing about the flowing emotions of his heart without censoring them. At the same time, he acknowledged that, in love, a woman and a man could unite as equals—a notion unheard of in the Arabic world then. In "A Paper to The Reader," he writes:

> In my red arteries, a woman
> walks with me within my folds
> She whispers and blows in my bones
> and turns my lungs into an oven
> Sex is what I carry in my core
> coming from the coasts of the primal

> My body hungers for another
> extends my hand to another
> Do you think you are separate from me?
> We are one person, one being
> united in one entity
> Your beauty comes from me. Without each other,
> neither exists. Nor does your beauty.

Qabbani also sought to shed light on the discrepant treatment of men's and women's sexuality. Men freely pursued pleasure, for which women were persecuted severely. In "Prostitution," Qabbani gives a voice to an adulterous woman:

> If a woman sins, she is interrogated.
> How many bloody predators are left alone?
> One bed joined them:
> The man is protected, and the woman falls.

The reaction from the religious and conservative community in Syria was severe. Qabbani was attacked not only by political and religious authorities but also by people on the streets. Women who were not allowed to leave their houses threw garbage on him when he walked down the narrow alleys of Damascus. Community leaders met with his father to express their outrage and warn him that threats were issued to kill his son or prosecute him. Women's neighbors advised his mother to solicit the Sheiks' advice to exorcise the "Devil" inside him and "cure" him.

Though hungry and oppressed under the rules of the French colonizer for nearly thirty years (1919-1948), the Syrian people replaced their pursuit of independence and dignified existence in their own country with attacking a 28-page book of poems and its author. In his autobiography, Qabbani described the reaction to his first collection:

> In a second, history moved, and the historians moved; they
> rejected the book, its sentences, and its details. They rejected

its title and theme and even its cover. They attacked me viciously as if they were injured beasts. My flesh was then soft, and their knives were sharp. And the celebration of stoning me started. (*My Story with Poetry*. Nizar Qabbani Press, 2000. p.93).

But none of this deterred Qabbani from his quest to liberate love from the chains of denial and the strangulation of oppression. He took some comfort in the better reception of the book by the more modern neighboring Lebanon. Qabbani drew strength from young, Western-minded readers and energy from letters of praise and appreciation sent in secrecy by a young generation of oppressed women yearning for freedom.

His dedication to resisting the strangulation of love was inspired by his older sister, Wisal, with whom he had a close relationship. Their father had forced her to marry a man he had chosen instead of the man she loved. That she dared to even know a man outside the house's walls violated an absolute prohibition within the Syrian families. At the age of 15, she committed suicide.

After finishing high school, Qabbani decided to enroll in law school primarily to please his parents and secondly to have a job that could provide a living. His vision came to fruition when the French League of Nations Mandate ended in 1948. The newly independent nation of Syria was looking for an articulate and educated younger generation to represent the country and establish a national identity. Despite the previous grievances with his work, Nizar Qabbani was sent as a diplomat to work with the Syrian embassy in Egypt, where he served from 1945 to 1948.

Cairo provided Qabbani with a somewhat more open society than Damascus did. Egypt's connection to the West through colonialism under England from 1882-1952 allowed for a larger free space for the intellectuals to explore and debate. But still, Qabbani's provocative poems continued to be attacked by the religious leaders in Cairo. Ali Tantawi, a famous and influential Egyptian writer, called him "the poet of lust":

> [The book] describes the loose prostitutes and the sex workers realistically and without imagination because its author has no wide imagination, but he is a spoiled rich school boy. (*"Articles in Brief,"* Al-Rissala, no. 661, March 4, 1946).

Despite being content and somewhat free in Cairo, Qabbani longed for the world he lived in within the walls of his Damascus house: the open courtyard with the water fountain, the sound of water, the flowers, the trees, the roses, the jasmines, the birds, the world that nourished him as a child and a teen. He explained later that this world inside his house captured his imagination and sense of adventure and that he felt no need to leave it and go outside like other kids did (*My Story with Poetry*, p. 33).

Nizar tried to reconcile his two competing worlds: the world of traditional social mores (including his close relationship with his parents and his civic service) with the world of poetry, his imagination, and fantasies. Conflicted, he sometimes had to submit to one or the other of those forces. His loneliness in Cairo forced him to submit to his parents' wish to marry a woman of their choosing, who became his first wife, Zahra. They would soon have two children, Toufic and Hadbaa.

THE CHILDHOOD OF A BREAST (1947)

In 1947, in Egypt, Qabbani produced his second book of poems, *The Childhood of a Breast*. And once again, the mere title provoked outrage in the Arab world. When a journalist friend of Qabbani wrote a review of the book pre-publication, the journal's editor would not publish the review unless the title was changed to *The Childhood of a River*. The words 'breast' and 'river' in Arabic rhyme and share the same initial letters; only the last letter is different:

nahed (breast) and *naher* (river). The friend agreed, but Qabbani was furious; he rejected the proposal and insisted on publishing the book with the original title despite all criticism.

The Childhood of a Breast received a good review from the liberal literary scene in Lebanon and the younger literary critics. Qabbani's resistance to oppression and the silencing of love had started making headway in the Arab world, especially among a younger generation aspiring for a more open society.

The book chronicles his experiences with women, both actual and invented. His long line of admirers (especially women) and unapologetic narratives created a wedge of disapproval and discomfort between him and his wife, leading to their mutual disappointment. About marriage, Qabbani laments in the famous verses: "The priest / is the cook / who turns beautiful love relationships / to frozen fishes."

Qabbani's second collection was as provocative as the first. In his introduction to the book, he declared his intent to make his poetry accessible to everyone and posited that poetry is a necessity of life:

> If the reader feels that their heart is replaced with mine, and it started jumping within their ribcage; that they knew me before they knew about me; and that I became their mouth and voice, then I would know that I have achieved my white dream, which is to put poetry in every house, like bread and water. (The Childhood of a Breast. p.8)

In this second collection of poems, Qabbani reiterated and reaffirmed his commitment to freedom against the constraints of moral criticism. In his poem "Whispers," he wrote: "As long as you are mine / I care not about what they might have said / or what is going to be said about us."

He also continued to celebrate the beauty of the woman's body, combined with nature's beauty. Although his verses discomfited some readers, other readers longed for more, for someone who expressed what they wished but could not have. In his poem "Nipple," he praises the nipple as:

> A whispered word, written with light
> Brown or red
> its color is my emotions running barefoot
> in a lush meadow
> Or is it a kiss frozen on your breast?

Although Qabbani's poetry started to receive some recognition in the Arab world, his eyes were on the West. He longed for literary freedom away from the restrictions and the struggles against Middle Eastern social and moral values. His pull towards the West started in *Turkey*, where he was assigned a post in the Syrian Embassy, and he was delighted. At that time, Turkey was becoming a more secular Westernized state and thus satiated Qabbani's curiosity for adventure and discovery.

YOU ARE MINE (1950)

While in Ankara in 1950, Qabbani published his third poetry collection, *You Are Mine*, which included recollections of his visits to Lebanon during the summer. But in addition to his renowned adoration of women's beauty, Qabbani brought out the falsehood, betrayal, and dark sides of sexual encounters, including his own. In his poem "A Cat":

> I hate her, but I desire her
> and I love my hate for her.
> [...]
> The devil resides in her eyes
> and her lust blinded her mind.
> [...]
> If she embraces me, she will break my ribs
> and empty the poison of her mouth into mine

> I love my hate for her
> and I wish when I hug her to kill her.

Qabbani's post in Turkey ended in 1951, after which he came back to Damascus and spent an unsettling year there. His marriage was falling apart, and he was conflicted between reconciling with his wife or ending their marriage. Divorce was unpopular and stigmatized in Syria. However, the couple recognized that their separation was inevitable and they finalized their divorce in 1952.

That same year, Qabbani was offered a post in the Syrian embassy in London. He accepted it without hesitation. The move came at the perfect time to escape the troubling personal and social conflicts he was enduring, and England was the dream of experiencing the West he had always longed for.

The London Years

Qabbani's three years in England have proven to be beneficial to his personal growth and the maturity of his poetry. In London, Qabbani tasted freedom away from the restrictions and taboos of the Arab world; he thrived in the progressive West after being hostage to the regression of the Middle East. In a letter to his friend, he admitted that England "washed away his desert's dust" and that there, he experienced "literary security." In England, Qabbani learned and mastered English. He read Western literature widely. He also appreciated and delved into the philosophical movements of the time, especially Existentialism. In his poem "Existentialist," he writes:

> She is an existentialist
> because she is alive
> she wants to choose what she sees
> wants to tear up life
> because she loves it so

Qabbani believed that he wrote some of his best poems in London, poems that were more in touch with humanity. Although Qabbani continued to write about women, his writing expanded from celebrating love and beauty to addressing female subjugation in a predominantly patriarchal society. Qabbani's poems took on the spirit of activism and brought about subjects that were never discussed before. It was unthinkable to talk about pregnancy out of wedlock, but he did so in the persona of a woman in his poem "Pregnant":

> What? You spit me out,
> and the vomit in my throat destroys me,
> and the fingers of nausea strangle me.
> Your doomed child is inside my body
> and the shame flattens me
> and a dark reality fills me.
> I am pregnant.

He also gave women a voice to rail against unfaithfulness in "Letter to An Angry Woman":

> You invited your mistress and humiliated me
> after I was the light of your eyes.
> I see her there next to the fireplace. She took my seat there
> in that corner, that chair.

More importantly, Qabbani tried to point out to women that their lower social status results from being dependent on men. In the voice of a male, he says in "To A Worker":

> With my money
> and not with pleasant conversations
> you destroy your dignity, with my money
> and what it buys of precious things and dreamy silk.
> You obeyed me and followed me
> like a blind cat, believing in everything I claim.

To awaken his people—so they could see and comprehend their plight—became his mission in poetry. The poem became his weapon against backwardness and idiocy. The peak of this role came with his 1955 poem, "Bread, Hashish, and the Moon," published in the progressive journal Al-Adib (The Author). The journal was published in Lebanon and was known for running poems and articles too daring for other journals to accept.

> On Middle Eastern nights
> when the moon is full
> the Middle East sheds its dignity
> and its will to toil
> The millions who run without shoes
> and believe in four wives
> and the day of judgment
> The millions who find bread
> only in dreams
> and live at night in houses loud with coughing
> —they've never known what medicine is

The poem angered the conservative leaders in the Arab world, especially Damascus's religious authorities. They demanded this poem be discussed in the Parliament and that Qabbani should be discharged from his diplomatic post, calling him a traitor and a disgrace to his country and religion. However, the Parliament refused to vote and left any repercussions to the foreign minister, who stood by Qabbani and advised the offended religious group to write a counter poem to respond to Qabbani's criticism. Nevertheless, the climate was so hostile against him in Damascus that his brother, out of fear for his life, advised him to delay coming back from England until things calmed down.

Poems (1959)

Qabbani came back to Damascus to find the political climate more volatile. Many political parties were emerging in Syria. Egypt had just gotten rid of its king and taken on nationalizing its Suez Canal. The move gained President Gamal Abdel Nasser's unprecedented support across the Arab world and angered France, England, and Israel. In 1959, Qabbani published his book *Poems*, which included the collection he had written while in London.

Qabbani had tried to stay away from politics and write for the art itself. However, when the climate of animosity between Israel and its neighboring Egypt and Syria led to military confrontations, Qabbani found himself moved and pressured to put his poetry and popularity in the service of his nation. His poem, "I Write for The Children," invoked a sense of nationalism and was welcomed on the front pages of many journals:

> They came to our small homeland
> our peaceful, small homeland
> dirtied our soil
> executed our women
> made our children orphans
> And the United Nations
> is still looking into the matter of the free nations and their sovereignty.

In Damascus, Qabbani met the author Colette Khouri, and he fell passionately in love with her. Their relationship was frowned upon in conservative Damascus not only because she was Christian and he was Muslim, but, as importantly, they were unmarried. Both situations violated some of the most stringent social prohibitions in the Arab world. His passion for Colette Khouri produced a wealth of romantic poetry that was later collected in his book, *My Beloved*, published in 1959. In "When It Rains Turquoise," Qabbani describes his lover's eyes: "Two rivers from tobacco and honey / Even the sun is unlike them / Curtains—if they move / I see the face of God behind them."

However, their relationship was complicated and frustrating to him. Colette Khouri was unlike the other women he knew; she was his equal intellectually, lived a liberal life, and traveled extensively. She was not going to be imprisoned by his passion and be only his. Despite his ardor, he flirted with other women during her lengthy trips to Europe or the USA, which angered her and created tension between them. When he was assigned a post in China in 1958 for a year, he thought it would be a timely break from the intensity of their relationship.

Cold China

Under the austerity of communism, China proved to be depressing and uninspiring to his creativity. His writing during that time was morbid and melancholic. There, he wrote his 65-page poem, "Diary of an Indifferent Woman." His verses voiced helplessness that approached suicidal ideas as cold China brought back to him the memories of his sister's suicide. In the poem, he unloaded his bitterness against the social mores and family pressure that rendered life a burden for his sister and many like her.

> My days are repetitive
> boring like the ticking of the clock
> How did my femininity die? I don't remember
> My summer is not a summer
> and my flowers don't blossom
> What would interest me?
> Is there anything inside me that wasn't destroyed?
> Do I care about the mold surrounding me
> or the values that I reject?
> My life is useless
> there is no news that I live for or a messenger

For no one, I live
and nothing I wait for.

The poem was prefaced with those famous five lines that continue to be repeated on the tongue of every girl and woman in the Arabic world till now:

Revolt! I would love for you to revolt
Revolt against the East of slaves and incense and concubines
Revolt against history, and triumph over the big illusion
Don't be afraid. The sun is the eagles' cemetery
Revolt against the East who sees you as a feast over a bed

BACK TO THE TURMOIL

Qabbani's mission in China ended in 1960, and he returned to Damascus. At that time, Syria and Egypt were still unified under the United Arab Republic, which was established in 1958. The Syrians initially welcomed the union, but later, they grew impatient with Cairo's dominance and with the marginalization of Syria's power. The union ended in 1961.

At the same time, Saudi Arabian oil made the Saudi Sheiks and their families very wealthy. Some of them threw their endless source of wealth at the feet of women and mistresses and traveled to Europe to find the pleasures they could not have in their homeland. Qabbani was outraged by that new trend, and he denounced such use of oil wealth in his famous poem, "Love and Petroleum":

O the prince of oil, soak in the mud of your pleasures
Soak like a cleaning sponge in your ignorance
You have the oil; squeeze it on your mistresses' feet
The nights' caves in Paris killed your honor
There, under the feet of prostitutes, you buried your revenge
You sold Jerusalem and God. You sold the ashes of your dead

In 1962, Qabbani traveled to Iraq to read poetry at the University of Baghdad. There, he met his future wife, Balqis. She captivated Qabbani's attention immediately. She was 22 years old, with green eyes and long blond hair and she was educated and passionate about poetry. Their conversation intrigued him, and he was entertaining the prospect of marrying her at the end of his trip. However, being from a prominent Iraqi family, her father was opposed to their relationship because of Qabbani's reputation and the father's knowledge of the theme of his poems. But, with the instinct and the vision of a poet, Qabbani knew that Balqis was going to be his wife, and it was just a matter of time. In "The Cost of My Poetry," he says:

> "She's in love with a poet,"
> the women of the old city
> chew up our great story
> and men raise their arms and make a fist
> and glasses knock down glasses
> as if, as if it is a crime
> that you love a poet

ANDALUSIA

Shortly after returning to Damascus, Qabbani was assigned to serve in the Syrian embassy in Madrid, Spain, from 1962-1966, a post he was looking forward to. In Spain, Qabbani felt less alienated than in any other place in Europe. The influence of the Arabic ruling of the land for seven centuries (711-1492) made Spain feel like a home away from home. In addition, the Syrian ambassador and his family provided him with a welcoming friendship. There, he learned Spanish and emerged into Spanish art and culture: literature, music, theater, and all. Some 30 of his poems were translated into Spanish and published in Spanish journals when he was there.

Back in Damascus, the political atmosphere was still unstable. The Ba'ath political party had taken control, and the changes in the governing body had reached Spain. His friends, the ambassador, and his wife were let go, and a favorite of the Party replaced them. Although Qabbani was saved in his post, the conflict that he always felt between the mask he had to wear as a diplomat and the poet in him has awakened again. From Spain, he wrote the emotional poem "Five Letters to My Mother": "Two years had passed, Mother / and the face of Damascus / is a bird scratching our souls / biting our curtains / and pecking our fingers."

More and more, Qabbani felt that his poetic being was being suppressed and censored because of his work with the Syrian government, and he started contemplating leaving his job and dedicating his time to writing poetry. In 1966, Qabbani turned in his resignation as he came back to Damascus. And that ended his career as a Diplomat.

Nizar, the publisher

When Qabbani came back from Spain in 1966, he made Beirut, Lebanon, his home. Beirut was the cultural capital of the Arabic world. It was called the Paris of the East, where free expression was allowed without prosecution.

Beirut was a welcomed homecoming for Qabbani. There, his early poems had found an audience and admirers. In Beirut, Nizar started his publishing house, Nizar Qabbani Press, and he published his book *Painting with Words*. The collection contained 54 poems and included those he wrote in Spain. In these poems, he summarizes his past and his new direction: denouncing the patriarchal male figure in the Middle East and announcing the end of that era in his mind. He speaks in the person of Haroun Al-Rashid, the famous Caliph who was known for his relentless pursuit of women and pleasure:

> Today, I sit on my ship
> like a thief looking for a way out
> I turn the key to the women's room
> I only see skulls in the shadow
> Where are the concubines I owned?
> Where is the incense lost from my chamber?
> Today, the breasts avenge themselves
> and return my stabbing with stabs.

On June 5, 1967, the Arabs were defeated by Israel in the Six-Day War. As a result, they lost Sinai in Egypt, the West Bank in Jordan, and the Golan Heights in Syria. The defeat shook the Arab thinkers and writers, including Qabbani. The poem he wrote then, "Notes on The Book of Defeat," marks the shift in Qabbani's direction from writing about love and women to political activism: "O my sad nation / You turned me in a second / from a poet who wrote about love and longing / to a poet who writes with a knife." In this poem, Qabbani blamed the Arab world's culture and leaders for the defeat:

> We lost the war, and that is no wonder
> because we entered it
> with our Oriental talent for making speeches
> with our bravado that never killed a fly
> Because we entered it
> with the logic of the drum and the rebab

The poem angered the Arab world in general and Egypt in particular. He and his poems were banned from entering Egypt. The Arabic radios stopped airing the songs whose lyrics were some of his poems. Eventually, the ban was lifted after Qabbani sent a personal letter to Nasser, the president of Egypt, explaining the source of his nationalist passion that triggered the poem. And Nasser, in turn, ordered that ban to cease.

Qabbani's reputation and popularity among intellectuals soared after his controversial poem. He was given a column in the Mawaqef journal where Qabbani published one of his most daring poems, "The Interrogation." He criticized the rigidity of the traditional oppressive Islamic leadership. The following verses are in the voice of a faithful Muslim who killed his Imam: "With my dagger, the one you see, / I stabbed him / in his neck and chest / I stabbed him / in his brain, rotten like wood / I stabbed him in my name / and the name of the millions of sheep."

A Husband Again

On a personal note, through letters, Qabbani was still in contact with Balqis in Iraq. Their relationship was getting more robust with time. In 1969, Qabbani traveled to Baghdad to attend the poetry festival, and he took that opportunity to try again for her hand in marriage. Balqis and her parents attended the festival where Qabbani read his poem, "Testimony in the Court of Poetry." In the poem, Qabbani expressed his gratitude to Baghdad, hinting at his problem with Balqis's father, who rejected their marriage. He says, "I am coming to you, and my heart / is a white dove on my palm / Understand me; I am a child/evening washes over his eyes / Centuries of sorrows live inside me / Do I have a refuge in Iraq?" The poem was a great success and was talked about in political and intellectual circles. Thus, Qabbani found the courage to ask a highly ranked politician to appeal to Balqis' father to accept his marriage proposal, and it worked.

Qabbani and Balqis married, and they went back together to Beirut. His years with Balqis were the happiest and most productive; he then published three collections: *The Book of Love*, *Wild Poems*, and *One Hundred Letters of Love*. And later, in 1973, he published his collection, Poems Against the Law. Balqis gave Qabbani one daughter and one son: Zeineb and Omar.

TRAGEDIES

In 1973, Qabbani's eldest son from his first marriage, Tawfic, died of a heart condition while in medical school. Qabbani lamented the loss of his son in "To The Damascene Prince:"

> O Tawfik
> If Death had a child
> it would have known what the death of a child means
> If it had a mind
> we would have asked it to explain the death of Bulbuls and Jasmines
> If it had a heart
> it would hesitate before it slaughters our dear children.

After the death of his son, Qabbani's poetry production slowed, and he spent more time writing a column for the *Al-Ousboo Al-Arabi* (*The Arabic Week*) magazine. His writing was focused on encouraging an Arabic cultural and political revolution. Qabbani's health conditions were not the greatest, and in 1974, Qabbani suffered a heart attack, from which he recovered.

The early signs of a civil war in Beirut started in 1975 when one act of militia terror led to another. Out of fear for their safety, Qabbani took his family to Baghdad. During the year he spent there, he continued to express his unshaken feeling that he had abandoned his lover, Beirut. Qabbani returned to Beirut from what he called an exile to Iraq and went back to writing for the journal and running his publishing house despite the ongoing civil war. In 1978, Qabbani published his collection, *To Beirut, the Female, with Love*. In this collection, he portrayed his love for Beirut and compared her pain and wound to that of an oppressed and violated woman: "O Beirut, the lady of the world / Who sold your ruby bracelets? / Who confiscated your magic ring / and cut your golden braids?"

Beirut, however, took the woman he loved. In 1981, the Iraqi embassy—where Balqis worked—was bombed by a Shiite extremist group called Al-Dawa. Balqis died in the explosion. Her loss devastated Qabbani, who mourned her in his poem "Balqis," in which he accused all the Arabic regimes of her murder:

> I am going to say during the interrogation
> that I know the names and the things and the prisoners
> and the martyrs and the poor and the oppressed
> And I am going to say that I know the executioner who
>   killed my wife
> and the faces of all the investigators
> And say that our chastity is adultery
> and that our piety is dirtiness
> And say our struggle is a lie
> and that there is no difference
> between politics and prostitution

Shortly after Balqis' death, Qabbani had another heart attack and needed a bypass surgery, which he had done in the United States.

THE YEARS IN BETWEEN

With Beirut burning with the civil war and Balqis dead, Qabbani was looking for a place to go. Syria was in turmoil as the regime was cracking down on the Muslim Brotherhood of Islam political party. Qabbani wanted to go to Cairo, but Cairo was no longer a welcoming place to him, with the conservative Islamic movements taking more control.

His savior was Princess Souad, a Kuwaiti poet with a doctoral degree in political economy from England. They had developed a close relationship and started traveling together to Europe. The only problem was that Princess Souad was married to a Kuwaiti sheik and had children. But Qabbani was not apologetic; he announced his love publicly in "The Decision":

> I love you without reservation
> I live my birth in you, and my destruction
> I committed myself to you voluntarily and on purpose
> If I were a shame, how glorious this shame!
> What and who in the world would scare me?

Qabbani spent the next few years traveling between Beirut and Europe with Princess Souad and alone. He continued to write his love poems: at that point, they were to Souad, and he also continued to instigate rebellion and revolt against the oppressive Arab climate. In "Top Secret Report from the Land of Oppression," he says:

> Because of this, I announce my rebellion
> in the name of the masses sitting like cows
> under the little screens
> in the name of the masses who are being fed submission
> with a large spoon
> in the name of the masses who are ridden like mules
> from dawn to sunset.

After three years of shuttling between Beirut and different European cities, he decided to settle in Geneva. There, he wrote such politically provocative poems that the Syrian secret service was sent to break into his house as an act of intimidation. In his poem, "Words in the Fangs of the Secret Service," he writes:

> They finally came
> My heart always told me
> they would come
> to arrest the word or me
> so, they did not surprise me
> They broke the door of my house in Geneva

> They soiled the snow of Switzerland
> and its grassland and its flocks of pigeons
> and they challenged the land of love and the bible of peace
> They placed my hair in bags
> Did you see them?
> A nation steals the scent of jasmine
> what a joke!
> They stole my ink and my papers
> but they did not steal the fire under my forehead
> I live in the people's memory
> What are they if they steal me?

But none of these threats fazed or disrupted Qabbani. In 1988, he visited Damascus to partake in a poetry festival at the National Library. The auditorium was packed, and loudspeakers were placed outside for the people gathered there to hear him. Boldly and without fear, Qabbani read "Memoir of an Arabic Executioner," spoken in the persona of the executioner:

> People, if I take off my mask, you would know me
> I am Genghis Khan; I came to you
> with my spears, my dogs, and my prisons
> Don't complain about my aggression
> I kill so you won't kill me
> I hang so you won't hang me
> I bury you in mass graves so that you won't bury me.

Qabbani went back to Geneva, leaving his voice and lines reverberating in the consciousness of the people who read him or heard him. There, he wrote seven more collections between 1987 and 1990.

London to the End

Qabbani's daughter, who lived in London, had implored him to move from Geneva to London to stay close to her, which he finally did in 1990.

Shortly after Qabbani settled in London, Saddam Hussein of Iraq invaded his neighboring Kuwait. Although the move was encouraged by many of the Arab world's leaders, Qabbani was furious about it and vociferous. He wrote a poem he titled after his previous famous 1967 poem, "Notes in the Book of Defeat," and added 1991 to the title. In the new poem, he wrote:

> Every twenty years,
> a ruler comes to us
> and guillotines the Sun itself
> Every twenty years
> a gambling man comes to us
> to pawn the nations, the people, the heritage
> to risk the sunrise and sunset
> our men and women
> the very waves of the sea itself
> on the gambling table.

Qabbani witnessed firsthand what his daring poetry had done to shake people and nations. When he traveled to Algeria for a poetry reading, the Islamic opposition took to the streets and protested against allowing him to take the stage. He was threatened with violence. The event was canceled, and he flew back to London.

During those years, Qabbani made a few visits to Beirut for readings. He continued to write about women, many of whom were his prior lovers who had become close friends. He also continued to critique what he saw as a deficiency and plague in Arabic thinking. In "When Will They Announce the Death of the Arabs," he voices his frustration with the static status of the Arab world:

"I traveled north, I traveled south / all useless / the coffee tastes the same in all shops / all women, when naked smell, the same /all the men in the tribes don't chew their food / but in a second, they devour women."

Qabbani had devoted much of his poetry to ridiculing and destroying the traditional sexual codes. But those codes continued to prevail despite his efforts, popularity, and women's recognition that his work had opened their eyes to a new possibility of freedom. In the end, Qabbani made peace with living in exile and romanticized it. "In Good Morning Exile," he said, "I don't feel estranged in my Exile any longer / I don't complain about the harsh exodus / Exile is my dear friend now / he comes to drink coffee with me / and read the newspaper."

In London, Qabbani published six more collections of poems, the last in 1998, *The Alphabet of Jasmine*. In the same year, Qabbani got ill and spent time in the hospital in London, where he later died. Following the provisions of his will, Qabbani was buried in Damascus.

In a poem he had addressed to the people of Damascus, he had said:

I am your Damascene flower, O people of Damascus
He who finds me should put me in a vase
I am your mad poet, O people of Damascus
He who finds me should take a photograph of me
I am your homeless moon, O people of Damascus
He who sees me should give me a bed and a cover
for I haven't slept in centuries.

Rest in peace, Mr. Qabbani. Your home is in the heart of all people.

Love and Resistance

I love you to lift up the sky
to regain my wellbeing
and the wellbeing of my words
and to free myself of the pollution
that strangles my heart

— Nizar Qabbani

Why I Write

I write
to blow things to smithereens, and writing is an explosion
I write
for the light to triumph over darkness
and the poem is a triumph
I write
for the wheat stalk to read me
and the trees to read me
for the flower and the star and the bird
and the fish and the cat and the shell and the oyster
to understand me

I write
to save the world from the teeth of *Hulagu*
and the militia's rulers
and the gang leader's craziness
I write
to save women from the tyrant's dungeon
from the cities of death
from polygamy
from the similarity of the days
the freeze and the monotony
I write to save the word from the inquisition
from the dog's sniffing
from the noose of censorship

I write to save my lover
from non-poetry, from non-love
from frustration, from depression

لماذا أكتب

كي أفجّر الأشياء، والكتابة انفجار
أكتب
كي ينتصر الضوء على العتمة،
والقصيدة انتصار
أكتب
كي تقرأني سنابل القمح،
وكي تقرأني الأشجار
كي تفهمني الوردة، والنجمة، والعصفور،
والقطة، والأسماك، والأصداف، والمحار

أكتب
حتى أنقذ العالم من أضراس هولاكو
ومن حكم الميليشيات،
ومن جنون قائد العصابة
أكتب
حتى أنقذ النساء من أقبية الطغاة
من مدائن الأموات،
من تعدد الزوجات،
من تشابه الأيام،
والصقيع، والرتابة
أكتب
حتى أنقذ الكلمة من محاكم التفتيش
من شمشمة الكلاب،
من مشانق الرقابة

أكتب.. كي أنقذ من أحبها
من مدن اللاشعر، واللاحب، والإحباط، والكآبة

I write
to make her a prophet
an icon
a cloud

Nothing saves us from death except
the woman and writing
the woman and writing

Hulagu (c. 1217-1265): Genghis Khan's grandson. As part of the Mongol plan to subdue the Islamic world, Hulagu seized and sacked Baghdad, which was the religious and cultural capital of Islam. He defeated the caliph's army, captured and executed Al-Musta'sim, the last of the Abbasid caliphs, and then captured Syria. His conquests contributed to the decline and destruction of medieval Iranian culture.

أكتب.. كي أجعلها رسولةً
أكتب.. كي أجعلها أيقونةً
أكتب.. كي أجعلها سحابة

لا شيء يحمينا من الموت،
سوى المرأة.. والكتابة
سوى المرأة.. والكتابة

Maritime Poem

In the blue harbor of your eyes
the light rains out loud
and dizzy suns and sails
plan their ultimate voyage

In the blue harbor of your eyes
a window is open to the sea
and birds appear on the horizon
searching for unborn islands

In the blue harbor of your eyes
snow falls in July
and boats carrying turquoise
drown the sea, themselves undrowned

In the blue harbor of your eyes
I run on the rocks like a child
inhale the scent of the sea
and return an exhausted bird

In the blue harbor of your eyes
I dream of sailing on a hunt
for a million moons and
pearl necklaces and lilies

In the blue harbor of your eyes
stones speak in the dark
Who hid these thousands of poems
in the closed notebook of your eyes?

If I were, if I were a sailor
and someone gave me a boat
I would moor my sails every night
in the blue harbor of your eyes

القصيدَة البحريّة

في مرفأ عينيك الأزرق
أمطارٌ من ضوءٍ مسموع
وشموسٌ دائخةٌ.. وقلوع
ترسم رحلتها للمطلق

في مرفأ عينيك الأزرق
شبّاكٌ بحريٌ مفتوح
وطيورٌ في الأبعاد تلوح
تبحث عن جزرٍ لم تخلق

في مرفأ عينيك الأزرق
يتساقط ثلجٌ في تموز
ومراكبٌ حبلى بالفيروز
أغْرَقَتِ البحر ولم تَغْرَق

في مرفأ عينيك الأزرق
أركض كالطفل على الصخر
أستنشق رائحة البحر
وأعود كعصفورٍ مُرْهَق

في مرفأ عينيك الأزرق
أحلم بالبحر وبالإبحار
وأصيد ملايين الأقمار
وعقود اللؤلؤ والزنبق

في مرفأ عينيك الأزرق
تتكلم في الليل الأحجار
في دفتر عينيك المغلق
مَنْ خبّأ آلاف الأشعار؟

لو أني.. لو أني.. بحار
لو أحدٌ يمنحني زورق
أرسيت قلوعي كل مساء
في مرفأ عينيك الأزرق

I Love You to Lift Up the Sky

1

I love you to lift up the sky
to regain my wellbeing
and the wellbeing of my words
and to free myself of the pollution
that strangles my heart
For Earth without you
is a big lie—
a rotten apple

2

To enter the religion of Jasmine
and defend the civilization of poetry
To guarantee the blueness of the sea
and the greenness of the forests

3

I want to love you
to assure myself
that the palm trees in your eyes
are still okay
and the birds' nests in between your breasts
are still okay
and the fishes of poetry that swim in my blood
are still okay

أحبك حتى ترتفع السماء

1

كي أستعيد عافيتي
وعافية كلماتي
وأخرجُ من حزام التلوث
الذي يلُفّ قلبي
فالأرض بدونك
كذبةٌ كبيرة
وتفاحةٌ فاسدة

2

حتى أدخل في دين الياسمين
وأدافع عن حضارة الشعر
وزرقة البحر
واخضرار الغابات

3

أريد أن أحبك
حتى أطمئن أن غابات النخيل في عينيك
لا تزال بخير
وأعشاش العصافير بين نهديك
لا تزال بخير
وأسلاك الشعر التي تَسْبَح في دمي
لا تزال بخير

4

I want to love you
to banish my dryness
and saltiness
and the calcifications of my fingers;
to regain my springs
and my wheat stalks
and my colorful butterflies
and assure myself
that I can still cry

5

I want to love you
to retrieve the details of our Damascene house
each room
each tile
each pigeon;
to converse with the Arabian Jasmine
my mother used to behold every morning
like a jeweler would show off his jewels

6

My lady, I want to love you
in the time
of handicapped love
and handicapped language
and handicapped poetry books
when neither the trees can stand
nor the birds can use their wings
nor the stars can move around
without needing a visa

4
أريد أن أحبك
حتى أتخلص من يباسي
وملوحتي
وتتكلّس أصابعي
وأستعيد جداولي
وسنابلي
وفراشاتي الملونة
وقدرتي على البكاء

5
أريد أن أحبك
حتى أسترجع تفاصيل بيتنا الدمشقي
غرفةً... غرفة
بلاطةً... بلاطة
حمامةً... حمامة
وأتكلّم مع خمسين صفيحة فُل
كانت أمّي تستعرضها
كما يستعرض الصائغ جواهره

6
أريد أن أحبك، يا سيدتي
في زمن
أصبح فيه الحب معاقاً
واللغة معاقة
وكتب الشعر، معاقة
فلا الأشجار قادرةٌ على الوقوف على قدميها
ولا العصافير قادرةٌ على استعمال أجنحتها
ولا النجوم قادرةٌ على التّنقل
بدون تأشيرة دخول

7

I want to love you
before they capture the last free gazelle
and the last love letter
and before the last Arabic poem
is hung

8

I want to love you
before they announce a fascist decree
to close all the gardens of love
And I want to drink coffee with you
before they confiscate the coffee and the cups
And I want to sit with you for two minutes
before the Secret Service pulls the chairs from under us
And I want to hug you
before they arrest me and tie my arms and gag me
And I want to cry in your arms
before they tax my tears

9

I want to love you, my lady
to mount the carriage of time
and change the calendar
and rename the months and the days
and recalibrate the world clocks
with your footsteps
and with your scent
that enters the café before you

7

أريد أن أحبك
قَبْل أن ينقرضَ آخر غزالٍ
من غزلان الحرية
وآخر رسالةٍ
من رسائل المحبين
وتُشنَقُ آخر قصيدةٍ
مكتوبة باللغة العربية

8

أريد أن أحبك
قبل أن يَصْدُر مرسومٌ فاشستي
بإغلاق حدائق الحب
وأريد أن أتناول فنجاناً من القهوة معك
قبل أن يصادروا البنَّ والفناجين
وأريد أن أجلس معك.. لدقيقتين
قبل أن تَسْحَب الشرطة السرية من تحتنا الكراسي
وأريد أن أعانقك
قبل أن يلقوا القبض على فمي.. وذراعي
وأريد أن أبكي بين يديك
قبل أن يفرضوا ضريبةً جمركيةً
على دموعي

9

أريد أن أحبك، يا سيدتي
حتى أمتطي عربة الوقت
وأغيّر التقاويم
وأعيْد تسمية الشهور والأيام
وأضبط ساعات العالم
على إيقاع خطواتك
ورائحة عطرك
التي تدخل إلى المقهى
قبل دخولك

10

I love you, my lady
to defend the right of the horse
to neigh as loud and as long as it wishes;
and the right of the woman
to choose her knight
as she wishes;
and the right of the tree to change its leaves as it wishes
and the right of the people to change their leaders
as they wish

11

I want to love you
to return to Beirut its severed head
and to its sea, the blue coat
and to its poets, their burned notebooks
I want to return
to Tchaikovsky, his white swan
and to Paul Eluard, the key of Paris
and to Van Gogh, the sunflowers
to Aragon, Eliza's eyes
to *Qays Ibn Al-Mulawwah*,
the combs of *Layla Al-Amiriah*

12

I want you to be my lover
for the poem to triumph
over the silencer gun
and for the pupils to triumph
over the tear gas
and the roses to triumph
over the trampling feet of the police
and for the bookstores to triumph
over the weapons' factories

10

إني أحبك، يا سيدتي
دفاعاً عن حقّ الفرس
في أن تصهل كما تشاء
وحقّ المرأة.. في أن تختار فارسها
كما تشاء
وحقّ الشجرة في أن تغيّر أوراقها
كما تشاء
وحقّ الشعوب في أن تغيّر حكامها
متى تشاء

11

أريد أن أحبك
حتى أُعيْد إلى بيروت، رأسها المقطوع
وإلى بحرها، معطفه الأزرق
وإلى شعرائها.. دفاترهم المحترقة
أريد أن أعيْد
لتشايكوفسكي.. بجعته البيضاء
ولبول ايلوار.. مفاتيح باريس
ولفان كوخ.. زهرة (دوار الشمس)
ولأراغون.. (عيون إلزا)
ولقيس بن الملوّح
أمشاط ليلى العامرية

12

أريدك، أن تكوني حبيبتي
حتى تنتصر القصيدة
على المسدس الكاتم للصوت
وينتصر التلاميذ
على الغازات المسيلة للدموع
وتنتصر الوردة
على هرولة رجال البوليس
وتنتصر المكتبات
على مصانع الأسلحة

13

I want to love you
to regain the things that resembled me
and the trees that used to follow me
and the Damascene cat that used to scratch me
and the writing that used to write me
I want to open the drawers
where my mother hid her wedding ring
and her gold bracelets
and her Hegazi rosary
and the strand of my golden hair
she kept since I was born

14

Everything, my lady,
is comatose
The satellites triumphed over the poets' moon;
and the calculators
over the Song of Songs
over Lorca's poems and Mayakovsky
and Pablo Neruda

15

I want to love you, my lady
before my heart turns into a spare piece
sold in the pharmacy
because cardiologists in Cleveland Clinic
can now produce hearts like shoes— in bulk

13

أريد أن أحبك
حتى أستعيد الأشياء التي تشبهني
والأشجار التي كانت تتبعني
والقطط الشامية التي كانت تخرمشني
والكتابات.. التي كانت تكتبني
أريد.. أن أفتح كل الجوارير
التي كانت أمي تخبئ فيها
خاتم زواجها وأساورها الذهبية المبرومة
ومسبحتها الحجازية
وخصلة من شعري الذهبي
بقيَت تحتفظ بها
منذ يوم ولادتي

14

كل شيء يا سيدتي
دخل في (الكوما)
فالأقمار الصناعية
إنتصرت على قمر الشعراء
والحاسبات الالكترونية
تَفَوَّقتْ على نشيد الإنشاد
وقصائد لوركا وماياكوفسكي
وبابلو نيرودا

15

أريد أن أحبك، يا سيدتي
قبل أن يصبح قلبي
قطعة غيار تُباع في الصيدليات
فأطباء القلوب في (كليفلاند)
يصنعون القلوب بالجملة
كما تُصنع الأحذية

16

The sky, my love, is low now
and the clouds are strolling on the cement
And Plato's Republic
and Hammurabi's code
and the prophets' teaching
and the poets' words
are all below sea level now
The magicians and the astrologers
and the Sufi Sheikh
recommended that I love you to lift up the sky
a little bit

Qays Ibn Al-Mulawwah: A famous poet of the seventh century AD. He was known for writing love poems to *Layla Al-Amiriah*.

16

السماء يا سيدتي، أصبحت واطئة
والغيوم العالية
أصبحت تتسكع على الإسفلت
وجمهورية أفلاطون وشريعة حمورابي
ووصايا الأنبياء
وكلام الشعراء
صارَتْ دون مستوى سطح البحر
لذلك نصحني السحرة، والمنجمون،
ومشايخ الطرق الصوفية
أن أحبك
حتى ترتفع السماء قليلاً

African Breasts

Give me time
to welcome your love that came unannounced
Give me time
to remember this face that I had lost in the forest of forgetting
Give me time
to avoid this love that stops the blood in my arteries

Give me time
to learn your name
to learn my name
to learn where I was born and where I would die
and how I could be revived into a bird
to hide behind your eyelids
Give me time to study the winds
to learn the waves
and the map of all those bays

O woman who lives in what is coming
O the grains of pepper and pomegranates
Give me a country that makes me forget all countries

Give me time
to avoid this Andalusian face
to silence this Andalusian voice
to prevent this Andalusian death
and this sorrow that comes from everyplace
Give me time to prophesy the flood

O woman inscribed in volumes of magic
before you, the world was prose
but with you came poetry

نهد أفريقي

أعطيني وقتاً
كي أستقبل هذا الحب الآتي من غير استئذان
أعطيني وقتاً
كي أتذكر هذا الوجه الطالع من شجر النسيان
أعطيني وقتاً
كي أتجنب هذا الحب الواقف في نِصف الشريان

أعطيني وقتاً
حتى أعرف ما اسمك
حتى أعرف ما اسمي
حتى أعرف أين ولدتُ،
وأين أموت،
وكيف سأبْعَثُ عصفوراً بين الأجفان
أعطيني وقتاً
حتى أدرس حال الريح،
وحال الموج،
وأدرس خارطة الخلجان

يا امرأةً تسكن في الآتي
يا حبَّ الفلفل والرمان
أعطيني وطناً ينسيني كل الأوطان

أعطيني وقتاً
كي أتفادى هذا الوجه الأندلسي، وهذا الصوت الأندلسي،
وهذا الموت الأندلسي
وهذا الحزن القادم من كل مكان
أعطيني وقتاً يا سيدتي
كي أتنبأ بالطوفان

يا امرأة
كانوا كتَبوها في كتب السحر
من قبلك كان العالم نثراً
ثم أتيت فكان الشعر

Give me time
with your breast rearing like a horse
decisive like a period at the end of a sentence
Bedouin as cardamom, as coffee brewing over embers
perfectly forged like Damascene copper
majestic like Egyptian temples

I am interested in history
interested in finding an era
that can get me out of this one and put me in another
I am a Bedouin. I store wind in my lungs
I store the sun within my lips
and in my nerves, I store revenge
So break over the bed of love like a bottle of ink
and spread like an Indian perfume
I will be the flesh, and you the fingernails

Give me a chance
to catch the fish thrashing at your waist
The dance your feet weave on the carpet is a poem
and your hand over you belly eager for children is a poem
Give me a chance
to find the line between certainty and blasphemy

Give me a chance
to be sure of the stars
and the saints that spoke to me

O woman from whose thighs
—tall as palm trees in a desert—
white dates fall
Your breast speaks seven languages
give me time to learn them all

أعطيني وقتاً
كي أستوعب هذا النهد الراكض نحوي مثل المهر
كُرَويٌ نهدك مثل النقطة فوق السطر
بَدَوِيٌ.. مثل حبوب الهال،
ومثل القهوة فوق الجَمْر
وقديمٌ مثل نحاس الشام
قديمٌ مثل معابد مصر

وأنا مهتمٌ بالتاريخ،
وعصرٍ يُخرجُني من هذا العصر
وأنا بَدَوِيٌ.. أخزن في رئتي الريح،
وأخزن في شفتي الشمس،
وأخزن في أعصابي الثأر
فانكسري فوق سرير الحب، انكسري
مثل دواة الحبر
وانتشري.. كالعطر الهندي
فإني اللحم.. وأنت الظفر

أعطيني الفرصة
كي ألتقط السمك السابح تحت مياه الخصر
قدماك على وبر السجادة.. حالة شعر
ويداك.. على البطن المتحمس للأطفال،
قصيدة شعر
أعطيني الفرصة
كي أكتشف الحدَّ الفاصل بين يقين الحب
وبين الكفر

أعطيني الفرصة
حتى أقنع أني قد شاهدت النجم
وكلمني سيدنا الخضر

يا امرأةً.. يسقط من فخذيها البلح الأشقر
مثل النخلة في الصحراء
يتكلم نهدك سبع لغاتٍ
وأنا أحترف الإصغاء

O give me a chance
to avoid the rampaging storm of this love
the tornado of this love
this love with a wintery forecast

Give me a chance to be convinced, to believe, to be impious
to enter the flesh of things
Give me a chance to walk on water

Give me a chance to prepare
to enter the sea of your love
and dive in the salinity
burning from breast to navel
where sharks threaten to attack from everywhere
Give me a chance to breathe before I dive
into the seaweed of your arms
to read my future in your closed eyes
I am not used—my lady—to inhabit two men

O you with your African face
and squirrelly sad eyes
O woman, you are fuel and flame
you are the waving grass and its towering conflagration

Give me time to ready myself
to adapt
to adjust
to be sure of my passion

Give me ten minutes or five
to let the foam of love subside
to settle my nerves running wild

Give me little time to rest
At dawn, I will give you
my answer

أعطيني الفرصة
كي أتجنَّب هذا الحب العاصف،
هذا الحب الجارف
هذا الحب الشتوي الأجواء

أعطيني الفرصة حتى أقنع، حتى أؤمن، حتى أكفر
حتى أدخل في لحم الأشياء
أعطيني الفرصة.. حتى أمشي فوق الماء

أعطيني الفرصة
كي أتهيأ قبل نزول البحر
فكثيفٌ ملح البحر العالق بين السرة.. والنهدين
وكثيفٌ سمك القرش القادم.. لا أدري من أين
أعطيني الفرصة كي أتنفس
إن حشيش البحر خرافيٌ تحت الإبطين

أعطيني الفرصة
حتى أقرأ حظي في عينيك المغلقتين
فأنا سيدتي لم أتعوَّد
أن أتقمص في رَجلين

يا ذات الوجه الإفريقي، المأساوي، السنجاني
يا امرأةً تدخل في تركيب النار، وفي تركيب الأعشاب

أعطيني الفرصة كي أتهيأ
كي أتأقلم
كي أتعوَّد
كي أتأكد من ماهية إعجابي

أعطيني عشر دقائق.. خمس دقائق
حتى يهدأ زبد الجنس، وتهدأ حرب الأعصاب

أعطيني الفرصة كي أرتاح
وعند الفجر، سأعطيك جوابي

When I Love You

Earth swells when I love you
On your palms, all roads cross
and the stars redraw their intricate designs on mine
Fish multiply in the sea
and the moon circulates in my blood
My shape changes:
I become the trees
I become the rain
I become the black center of the Spanish eyes

Valleys and mountains form when I love you
Birth rates soar
Imaginary islands surface in your eyes
and people on Earth discover new planets
Wealth and passion rain on everyone
and God camping on the moon is content

When I love you, thousands of new words emerge—
a new language in a new city in a new country

The hours breathe faster and faster
Words fit together in ways they never did before:
Commas relax their curves
the feminine Arabic characters conceive children
and wheat sprouts from in between the pages
Birds from your eyes bring sweet hazel news
and from your breasts, come carnivals and Indian herbs
Mangoes fall into our laps, and forests flare-up in flame
and Nubian drums invade our dreams

حين أحبك

يتغيَّر – حين أحبك – شكل الكرة الأرضية
تتلاقى طرق العالم فوق يديك.. وفوق يديّ
يتغيَّر ترتيب الأفلاك
تتكاثر في البحر الأسماك
ويسافر قمرٌ في دورتي الدموية
يتغيَّر شكلي:
أصبح شجراً.. أصبح مطراً
أصبح أسودَ، داخل عين إسبانية

تتكون – حين أحبك – أوديةٌ وجبال
تزداد ولادات الأطفال
تَتَشكَّل جزرٌ في عينيك خرافية
ويشاهد أهل الأرض كواكب لم تخطر في بال
ويزيْد الرزق، يزيْد العشق، تزيْد الكتب الشعرية
ويكون الله سعيداً في حجرته القمرية

تَتَحضَّر – حين أحبك – آلاف الكلمات
تتشكل لغةٌ أخرى
مدنٌ أخرى
أمٌّ أخرى

تُسرع أنفاس الساعات
ترتاح حروف العطف.. وتحبل تاءات التأنيث
ويَنْبُت قمحٌ ما بين الصفحات
وتجيء طيورٌ من عينيك.. وتحمل أخباراً عسلية
وتجيء قوافلٌ من نهديك.. وتحمل أعشاباً هندية
يتساقط ثمر المانجو.. تشتعل الغابات
وتدق طبولٌ نوبية

The white sea—when I love you—fills with red flowers
and countries rise from the water
and countries slide under the water
My skin unfolds on three red roses and three white doves
The sun discovers womanhood and rises to wear her gold earrings
Bees migrate to your navel
And in between your breasts
all civilizations gather

Abbasid sorrows dwell in your eyes
and *Shiite cities* cry
and golden minarets gleam
and ancient mysteries reveal themselves
and my passion turns me into
Kufic scripts and designs

I stroll under the strands of your black hair
I read my nightly verses
I envision tropical islands and imaginary boats
bringing tobacco and oysters from the East Indies

When I love you, your breast breaks free from the submission
and turns into lightning, thunder, a sword, a sandstorm

All the Arabic cities—when I love you—protest
against centuries of oppression
against centuries of revenge
against the doctrines of all tribes

And I protest, when I love you, against the ugliness
against the *kings of salt*
and the institutions of the desert
And I will love you until the flood arrives
and I will love you until the flood arrives

يمتلئ البحر الأبيض – حين أحبك – أزهاراً حمراء
وتَلُوح بلادٌ فوق الماء
وتَغيب بلادٌ تحت الماء
يتغيَّر جلدي
تخرج منه ثلاث حماماتٍ بيضاء
وثلاث ورودٍ جورية
تكتشف الشمس أنوثتها
تضع الأقراط الذهبية
ويهاجر كل النحل إلى سرتك المنسية
وبشارع ما بين النهدين
تتجمَّع كلّ المدنية

يَسْتوطن حزنٌ عباسيٌ في عينيك
وتبكي مدنٌ شيعية
وتَلُوح مآذن من ذهبٍ
وتضيء كشوفٌ صوفية
وأنا الأشواق تحولني
نقشاً.. وزخارف كوفية

أتمشى تحت جسور الشعر الأسود
أقرأ أشعاري الليلية
أتخيَّل جزراً دافئةً
ومراكب صيدٍ وهمية
تَحمل لي تبغاً ومحاراً.. من جُزُر الهند الشرقية

يتَخلَّص نهدك – حين أحبك – من عقدته النفسية
يتحوَّل برقاً. رعداً. سيفاً. عاصفةً رملية

تتظاهر - حين أحبك – كلُّ المدن العربية
تتظاهر ضدَّ عصور القهر،
وضدَّ عصور الثأر،
وضدَّ الأنظمة القبلية
وأنا أتظاهر – حين أحبك – ضد القُبْح،
وضدَّ ملوك الملح،
وضدَّ مؤسسة الصحراء
ولسوف أظل أحبك حتى يأتي زمن الماء
ولسوف أظل أحبك حتى يأتي زمن الماء

Abbasid sorrows: Abbasid poetry is known for its sadness. In that era, the most famous poets (750-1258 AD) believed that life is all about pain and suffering. When Qabbani talks about the Abbasid sadness in the beloved's eyes, he refers to her recognition that living is to suffer.

The Shiite cities: Shia is a sect of Islam that worships and follows the teachings of the Imams (Hassan and Hussein). Traditionally, believers commemorate their deaths by going into the streets to cry loudly and beat their cheeks and chests to display their grief.

The kings of salt: In the Quran, there is a story of four kings who defeated their enemy and claimed that the geology of Palestine changed under their rule, such that the sea collapsed to form the salty Dead Sea. Here, Qabbani rebels against the claims that contradict science.

I Love You So Much

and I know that the road to the impossible is long
and I know that you are the queen among all women
and I don't have a choice
And I know the time of longing is gone
and the beautiful words have died

What do I say to the queen among all women
I love you so much

I love you so much, and I know that I live in one exile
and you live in another
and that between us there is wind
and clouds
and lightning
and thunder
and fire and snow
And I know that reaching your eyes is an illusion
and reaching you is a suicide
And it pleases me O precious
to tear myself apart for you
then put it back again
so I could love you a second time

O You who wove your shirt from the leaves of the tree
you who I protected from the drops of the rain
with infinite patience
I love you so much

And I know that I will travel in your eyes without certainty
and leave my mind behind me and run
run
run after my madness

أحبك جداً

وأعرف أن الطريق إلى المستحيل طويل
وأعرف أنك ستُّ النساء
وليس لدي بديل
وأعرف أن زمان الحنين انتهى
ومات الكلام الجميل

لِستِّ النساء ماذا نقول
أحبك جداً

أحبك جداً وأعرف أني أعيش بمنفى
وأنت بمنفى
وبيني وبينك
ريحٌ
وغيمٌ
وبرقٌ
ورعدٌ
وثلجٌ ونـار
وأعرف أن الوصول لعينيك وهمٌ
وأعرف أن الوصول إليك
انتحـار
ويسعدني
أن أمزِّق نفسي لأجلك أيتها الغالية
ولو خيروني
لكرَّرْتُ حبك للمرة الثانية

أيا من غَزلتُ قميصك من ورقات الشجر
أيا من حَميتكِ بالصبر من قطرات المطر
أحبك جداً

وأعرف أني أسافر في بحر عينيك
دون يقين
وأترك عقلي ورائي وأركض
أركض
أركض خلف جنوني

O Woman, you have my heart in your hands
never leave me, never
What would I be without your being?
I love you so much and much and much
I swear I'll never retire from your love
Is it even possible to retire from love?
What if I did?
What would I care
if I emerged from your love alive
And what would I care
if I emerged dead

أيا امرأةً تُمسِك القلب بين يديها
سألتك بالله لا تتركيني
لا تتركيني
فماذا أكون أنا إذا لم تكوني
أحبك جداً
وجداً وجداً
وأرفض من نــار حبك أن أستقيل
وهل يستطيع المتيم بالعشق أن يستقيل
وما همَّني إن خَرجتُ من الحب حياً
وما همَّني
إن خَرجتُ قتيلاً

Your Body Is My Map

Love me, then love me more
O the most beautiful fit of craze
O the dagger traveling in my cells
O the stabbing knife

Drown me more
for the sea is calling me
Kill me more
for if Death claims me, it may revive me

Your body is my map
The maps of the world concern me no longer
I am the oldest capital of love
and my wound is a pharaonic tattoo
My anguish spreads like an oil spill
from Lebanon to China
My anguish is a caravan
the Calif had sent from Damascus to China
in the seventh century
but it was lost
inside a dragon's mouth

O the bird of my heart, my April
O the ocean's sand, the olive forests
O the flavor of snow and the flavor of fire
O the taste of my suspicions and my certainties

I am afraid of the unknown; shelter me
I am afraid of the darkness; embrace me
I am cold; cover me
Read me children's stories
Stay with me

جسمك خارطتي

زيديني عشقاً.. زيديني
يا أحلى نوبات جنوني
يا سفر الخنجر في أنسجتي
يا غلغلة السكين
زيديني غَرَقاً يا سيدتي
إن البحر يناديني
زيديني موتاً
علَّ الموت، إذا يقتلني، يحييني

جسمك خارطتي.. ما عادَتْ
خارطةُ العالم تعنيني
أنا أُقَدَمُ عاصمةٍ للحب
وجرحي نقشٌ فرعوني
وجعي.. يمتدُّ كبقعة زيتٍ
من بيروت.. إلى الصين
وجعي قافلةٌ.. أرسلَها
خلفاءُ الشام.. إلى الصين
في القرن السابع للميلاد
وضاعت في فم تنين

عصفورة قلبي، نيساني
يا رمل البحر، ويا غابات الزيتون
يا طَعْم الثلج، وطعم النار
ونكهة شكّي، ويقيني

أشعر بالخوف من المجهول.. فآويني
أشعر بالخوف من الظلماء.. فضميني
أشعر بالبرد.. فغطيني
إحكي لي قصصاً للأطفال
وظلِّي قربي

Sing to me
I have been—since I was born—
looking for a home to rest my forehead
looking for a love that writes me on the walls and then erases me
for a love that can take me to the borders of the sun and leave me there

O the lilies of my life, my fan, my lantern, the confession of my meadows
Spread for me a bridge made of lemon fragrance
Wear me in the darkness of your hair like an ivory comb
and forget me
I am a wandering drop of water in the notebooks of October

Love me more and then more
O my most beautiful fit of craze
For you, I let go of all women
For you, I left my history behind me
I deleted my birth certificate
and I slit open all my arteries

غنّي لي
فأنا من بدء التكوين
أبحث عن وطنٍ لجبيني
عن حب امرأةٍ
يكتبني فوق الجدران.. ويمحيني
عن حب امرأةٍ.. يأخذني
لحدود الشمس ويرميني

نوّارة عمري، مروحتي
قنديلي، بَوح بساتيني
مدّي لي جسراً من رائحة الليمون
وضعيني مشطاً عاجياً
في عتمة شعرك.. وانسيني
أنا نقطة ماءٍ حائرة
بَقِيَتْ في دفتر تشرين

زيديني عشقاً زيديني
يا أحلى نوبات جنوني
من أجلك أعْتقت نسائي
وتركت التاريخ ورائي
وشطبت شهادة ميلادي
وقطعت جميع شراييني

The Book of Love

1

As long as you are, my green bird,
my love
God is in the sky

2

My lover asks me:
What is the difference between me and the sky?
The difference is
if you smile
I forget the sky

3

Love is a beautiful poem
written on the moon
Love is planted on the trees' leaves
Love is engraved
on birds' feathers and drops of rain
But in my country, if a woman loved a man
fifty stones would be thrown at her

4

When I fell in love
the kingdom of God changed:
Night slept in my coat
and the sun rose from the west

كتاب الحب

1

ما دمتِ يا عصفورتي الخضراء
حبيبتي
إذَنْ.. فإن الله في السماء

2

تسألني حبيبتي
ما الفرق ما بيني وما بين السماء؟
الفرق ما بينكما
أنكِ إن ضحكتِ يا حبيبتي
أنسى السماء

3

الحب يا حبيبتي
قصيدة جميلة مكتوبة على القمر
الحب مرسومٌ على جميع أوراق الشجر
الحب منقوشٌ على
ريش العصافير، وحبّات المطر
لكن أي امرأة في بلدي
إذا أحبَّتْ رجلاً
تُرمى بخمسين حجر

4

حين أنا سقطت في الحب
تَغيَّرْتُ
تَغيَّرَتْ مملكة الرب
صار الدجى ينام في معطفي
وتُشرق الشمس من الغرب

5

God, my heart is not large enough
The woman I love equals the world
So, place, in my chest, a heart
as large as the world

6

You're still asking me about my birthday
Write down then what you don't know:
the day my love for you was born is my birthday

7

If a genie emerges from the bottle and says:
"I am at your service;
you have one minute to choose
among emeralds or rubies."
I would—without hesitation—
choose your eyes

8

O, the one with black eyes
O, the one with the bright rainy eyes
I ask of God two things only:
to protect those eyes
and to make me live two more days
to write poetry about those two pearls

9

If you were, my friend,
on the level of my insanity
you would throw away your jewelry
and sell your bracelets
and sleep in my eyes

5

يا رب قلبي لم يعد كافياً
لأن من أحبها.. تعادل الدنيا
فضَعْ بصدري واحداً غيره
يكون في مساحة الدنيا

6

ما زلتَ تسألني عن عيد ميلادي
سَجِّل لديك إذَنْ.. ما أنت تجهله
تاريخ حبك لي.. تاريخ ميلادي

7

لو خرج المارد من قمقمه
وقال لي: لبَّيْك
دقيقة واحدة لديك
تختار فيها كل ما تريده
مِنْ قطع الياقوت والزمرد
لاخترتُ عينيك.. بلا تردد

8

ذات العينين السوداوين
ذات العينين الصاحيتين الممطرتين
لا أطلب أبداً من ربي
إلا شيئين
أن يحفظ هاتين العينين
ويزيد بأيامي يومين
كي أكتب شعراً
في هاتين اللؤلؤتين

9

لو كنت يا صديقتي
بمستوى جنوني
رميتِ ما عليك من جواهر
وبعتِ ما لديك من أساور
ونمتِ في عيوني

10

I complain about you to the sky
I complain about you to the sky
How did you, how,
summarize all the women in the universe?

11

Because the words of the dictionary died
because the words of the letters died
because the words of the novels died
I want to discover a way of passion
a way to love you without words

12

I did not tell them about you
but they saw you bathing in my eyes
I did not talk about you
but they read you in my ink and in my pages
Love has a scent
and how can the peach orchards not exude their fragrances

13

I hate to love like the others
and write like the others
I wish my mouth were a cathedral
and my letters were bells

14

I wrote about your love until
my pencils—blue, red, and green—
wore out, and all words ended
I fastened my passion to the pigeon's feet
I didn't know, my love,
that like pigeons, love flies

10
أشكوكِ للسماء
أشكوكِ للسماء
كيف استطعت، كيف، أن تختصري
جميع ما في الكون من نساء

11
لأن كلام القواميس مات
لأن كلام المكاتيب مات
لأن كلام الروايات مات
أريد اكتشاف طريقة عشق
أحبك فيها.. بلا كلمات

12
أنا عنك ما أخبرتهم.. لكنهم
لمحوك تغتسلين في أحداقي
أنا عنك ما كلمتهم.. لكنهم
قرأوك في حبري وفي أوراقي
للحب رائحةٌ.. وليس بوسعها
أن لاتفوح.. مزارع الدراق

13
أكره أن أحب مثل الناس
أكره أن أكتب مثل الناس
أودُّ لو كان فمي كنيسة
وأحرفي أجراس

14
ذَوَّبتُ في غرامك الأقلام
.. من أزرق.. وأحمر.. وأخضر
حتى انتهى الكلام
علّقتُ حبي لك في أساور الحمَام
ولم أكن أعرف يا حبيبتي
أن الهوى يطير كالحمَام

15

Count on your fingers with me:
First: you are my love
Second: you are my love
Third: you are my love
and fourth and fifth
and sixth and seventh
and eighth and ninth
and tenth: you are my love

16

Your love—O the deepest eyes
is an extremism
mysticism
worship
Your love is like
Birth and Death—
difficult to happen twice

17

Twenty thousand women I loved
Twenty thousand women I tried
but when I met you, my love,
I felt that I had just started

18

I reserved a room for two in the house of the moon
to spend the weekend, my love
The world's hotels don't please me
I want to stay at the moon
but there, my love,
they don't let visitors without women
Would you come with me, my moon, to the moon

15
عُدِّي على أصابع اليدين، ما يأتي
فأولاً: حبيبتي أنت
وثانياً: حبيبتي أنت
وثالثاً: حبيبتي أنت
ورابعاً وخامساً
وسادساً وسباعاً
وثامناً وتاسعاً
وعاشراً.. حبيبتي أنت

16
حُبُّك يا عميقة العينين
تطَرُّفٌ
تصَوُّفٌ
عبادة
حُبُّك مثل الموت والولادة
صعبٌ أن يعاد مرتين

17
عشرين ألف امرأة أحببت
عشرين ألف امرأة جرّبت
وعندما التقيت فيك يا حبيبتي
شعرتُ أني الآن قد بدأت

18
لقد حجزتُ غرفةً لاثنين في بيت القمر
نقضي بها نهاية الأسبوع يا حبيبتي
فنادقُ العالم لا تعجبني
الفندق الذي أحب أن أسكنه هو القمر
لكنهم هنالك يا حبيبتي
لا يقبلون زائراً يأتي بغير امرأة
فهل تجيئين معي
يا قمري.. إلى القمر

19

You can't escape me; I am your fate
You can't get rid of me; God has sent me to you
At times, I come out from your rabbit ears
and out of the bracelets in your hands at another
And when summer comes, my love,
I swim like a fish in the lake of your eyes

20

If you had remembered each word
I uttered in the last two years;
if I opened the thousandth letter
I wrote in the past two years,
we would have been in the sky of love—
two pigeons flying
and the one ring on your left hand
would have become two rings

21

Why, why when you became my lover,
did my ink light up, and the notebooks grew grass?
Things changed since you loved me
I became a child playing with the sun
I am not a prophet but
when I write about you, I become one

22–23

You are engraved on my hand
like Kufic lines on the mosque's wall;
engraved on the wooden chair, my love
and on the chair's arm
And every time you try to get away
for one minute,
I see you in the palm of my hand

19

لن تهربي مني فإني رجل مُقدَّرٌ عليك
لن تخلصي مني.. فإن الله قد أرسلني إليك
فمرَّة.. أطلع من أرنبة أذنيك
ومرَّة أطلع من أساور الفيروز في يديك
وحين يأتي الصيف يا حبيبتي
أسْبَحُ كالأسماك في بحرَتَيّ عينيك

20

لو كنتِ تذكرين كل كلمة
لفظتُها في فترة العامين
لو أفتح الرسائل الألف.. التي
كتبتُ في عامين كاملين
كنا بآفاق الهوى
طرنا حمامتين
وأصبح الخاتم في
إصبعك الأيسر.. خاتمين

21

لماذا.. لماذا.. منذ صرت حبيبتي
يُضيء مدادي.. والدفاتر تُعشب
تغيَّرت الأشياء منذ عشقتني
وأصبحتُ كالأطفال.. بالشمس ألعب
وأنا لست نبياً ورسلاً غير أنني
أصير نبياً.. عندما عنك أكتب

22-23

محفورة أنت على وجه يدي
كأسطر كوفية
على جدار مسجد
محفورة في خشب الكرسي.. يا حبيبتي
وفي ذراع المقعد
وكلما حاولت أن تبتعدي
دقيقة واحدة
أراك في جوف يدي

24

Don't be sad because the astronaut landed
on the moon
In my eyes
you are always
more beautiful than the moon

25

When I am in love
I am the king of time
I own Earth and what's on it
and I ride my horse straight into the sun

26

When I am in love
I turn kings into my subjects
and make China bow to my throne
and I move the seas to where I want them to be
and if I want, I can stop the seconds from ticking away

27

When I am in love
I become a liquified light
the eyes cannot see
And the poems in my notebook
turn into fields of mimosa and chrysanthemum

28

When I am in love
water flows from my fingers
and grass grows on my tongue
When I am in love
I become the time
beyond Time

24

لا تحزني
إن هبط الرواد في أرض القمر
فسوف تبقين بعينيَّ دائماً
أحلى قمر

25

حين أكون عاشقاً
أشعرُ أني ملِك الزمان
أمتلِك الأرض وما عليها
وأدخل الشمس على حصاني

26

حين أكون عاشقاً
أجعل شاه الفرس من رعيتي
وأخضِع الصين لصولجاني
وأنقل البحار من مكانها
ولو أردتُ أوقف الثواني

27

حين أكون عاشقاً
أصبح ضوءً سائلاً
لا تستطيع العين أن تراني
وتُصبح الأشعار في دفاتري
حقول ميموزا وأقحوان

28

حين أكون عاشقاً
تتفجَّر المياه من أصابعي
ويَنبُتُ العشب على لساني
حين أكون عاشقاً
أغدو زماناً خارج الزمان

29

I love you when you cry
I love your face, cloudy and gloomy
Sorrow binds and melts us together
I love those tears coming down
and I love the Fall that comes after they fall
Women are beautiful
but some are more beautiful when they cry

30-31

You misunderstood me, my friend
I don't have an emotional complex
and I am not Oedipus in my dreams and instincts
But every woman I have loved
I wanted her to be my mother and my lover
I wish with all my heart
that you become my mother

32

Everything they say about me is true
Everything they say about my reputation—
women and love—is true
But they do not know that I
—for your love—bleed like Christ

33

It happens that sometimes I cry like a child without a reason
It happens that I get bored of your soft eyes without a reason
It happens that I get tired of my words and of the papers in my books
It happens that I get tired of my tiredness

29

إني أحبك عندما تبكين
وأحب وجهك غائماً وحزين
الحزن يصهرنا معاً ويذيبنا
من حيث لا أدري ولا تدرين
تلك الدموع الهاميات أحبها
وأحب خلف سقوطها تشرين
بعض النساء وجوههن جميلة
تصير أجمل.. عندما يبكين

30-31

أخطأتِ يا صديقتي بفهمي
فما أعاني عقدة نفسية
ولا أنا أوديب في غرائزي وحلمي
لكن كل امرأة أحببتها
أردتُ أن تكون لي
حبيبتي وأمي
من كل قلبي أشتهي
لو تصبحين أمي

32

جميع ما قالوه عني صحيح
جميع ما قالوه عن سمعتي
في العشق والنساء قولٌ صحيح
لكنهم لم يعرفوا أني
أنزفُ في حبك مثل المسيح

33

يَحْدُثُ أحياناً أن أبكي
مثل الأطفال بلا سبب
يَحْدُثُ أن أسأم من عينيك الطيبتين
بلا سبب
يَحْدُثُ أن أتعب من كلماتي
من أوراقي من كتبي
يَحْدُثُ أن أتعب من تعبي

34

Your eyes are a rainy night;
my boat sinks in them
my writing is forgotten in them
Mirrors have no memory

35

I wrote on the wind
the name of the woman I love
I wrote it over water
I did not know that the wind
is not a good listener
and that water
doesn't memorize names

36

You still— even after you've traveled
since the age of ten—
planted
like the spear in my side

37

In honor of this face and these eyes,
spring visited twice this year
and the prophet visited us twice

38

I rain in your eyes like a cloud
I bring them a treasure of sadness and melancholy
In my suitcase
I carry a thousand streams
and a thousand, thousand forests
and I carry history under my coat
and I carry the alphabet

34
عيناك مِثل الليلة الماطرة
مراكبي غارقة فيها
كتابتي منسية فيها
إن المرايا ما لها ذاكرة

35
كتبتُ فوق الريح
اسم التي أحبها
كتبتُ فوق الماء
لم أدرِ أن الريح
لا تُحسِن الإصغاء
لم أدرِ أن الماء
لا يَحفظ الأسماء

36
ما زلتِ يا مسافرة
مازلتِ بعد السنة العاشرة
مزروعة
كالرمح في الخاصرة

37
كم مال هذا الوجه والعينين
قد زارنا الربيع هذا العام مرَّتين
وزارنا النبي مرَّتين

38
أهطل في عينيك كالسحابة
أحمل في حقائبي إليهما
كنزاً من الأحزان والكآبة
أحمل ألف جدول
وألف ألف غابة
أحمل التاريخ تحت معطفي
وأحرف الكتابة

39

The most wonderful thing about our love is
that it is illogical and brainless
The most beautiful thing about our love is
that it walks on water and doesn't drown

40

Don't worry—O the most beautiful of all
You may get older with the passing of years, but
as long as you are in my poems and my words
you will never grow older on my pages

41

It was not enough for you to be beautiful
you had to pass between my arms one day
to become beautiful

42

Every time I travel into your eyes, my love
I feel as if I were riding a magic carpet:
One pink cloud lifts me up
followed by a purple one
I spin in your eyes, my love
I spin as if I were Earth

43

How similar you are to a fish
quick in love like a fish
You killed one thousand women inside me
and you became the queen

39
أروع ما في حبنا أنه
ليس له عقل ولا منطق
أجمل ما في حبنا أنه
يمشي على الماء ولا يغرق

40
لا تقلقي. يا حلوة الحلوات
ما دُمْتِ في شعري وفي كلماتي
قد تكبرين مع السنين.. وإنما
لن تكبرين أبداً.. على صفحاتي

41
ليس يكفيك أن تكوني جميلة
كان لابد من مرورك يوماً
بذراعي
كي تصيري جميلة

42
وكلما سافرتُ في عينيك يا حبيبتي
أحسُ أني راكب سجادة سحرية
فغيمة وردية ترفعني
وبعدها.. تأتي البنفسجية
أدور في عينيك يا حبيبتي
أدور مثل الكرة الأرضية

43
كم تشبهين السمكة
سريعة في الحب.. مثل السمكة
قتلتِ ألف امرأة.. في داخلي
وصرتِ أنت الملكة

44

I am the messenger of love
I bring women my surprises
If I hadn't washed your breasts with wine
they would not be still alive
That your nipples are rounded
is the simplest of my miracles

45

The most beautiful thing about you is your insanity
The most beautiful thing, if you will,
is that your breasts break the law

46

Undress; it has been a long time
since miracles have fallen on Earth
Undress, undress
I am mute
and your body knows all languages

47

In the old days, your breasts
sang peace like a dove
How did your breasts overnight
become Judgment Day?

48

Stick your red fingernails in my neck
Don't be a sheep or a goat
When I come to you like a flaming volcano,
resist me with all your power
The most beautiful lips are those that rebel
and the worst are those that always submit

44

إني رسول الحب
أحمل للنساء مفاجآتي
لو أنني بالخمر.. لم أغسلهما
نهداك.. ما كانا على قيد الحياة
فإذا استدارت حلمتاك
فتلك أصغر معجزاتي

45

أجمل ما فيك هو الجنون
أجمل ما فيك، إذا سمحت
خروج نهديك على القانون

46

تَعَرّي.. فمنذ زمان طويل
على الأرض لم تسقط المعجزات
تَعَرّي.. تَعَرّي
أنا أخرس
وجسمك يعرف كل اللغات

47

كان نهداك.. في العصور الخوالي
يُنشدان السلام مثل الحمامة
كيف ما بين ليلة وضحاها
صار نهداك.. مثل يوم القيامة؟

48

ضعي أظافرك الحمراء.. في عنقي
ولا تكوني معي شاةً.. ولا حملاً
وقاوميني بما أوتيتِ من حيلٍ
إذا أتيتك كالبركان مشتعلاً
أحلى الشفاه التي تعصي.. وأسوأها
تلك الشفاه التي دوماً تقول: بلى

49

How I changed over a year!
I used to be interested in you naked
like a forest or a marble statue
Today, I only want you to be
a question mark

50

After every breakup, I say naively:
"This is the last woman;
this is the last time."
But I still fall in love again, a thousand times
and I die a thousand times
and I still say
"This is the last time."

51

Useless is what I write, my lady
My feelings transcend my language
My feelings towards you bypass my voice
Useless is what I write
As long as my words are more expansive than my lips
I will despise my writing
My problem is that you are my problem

52

Because my love for you is above words
I've decided to stay silent, and that is that

49

كم تغيرتُ بين عام وعام
كان همّي أن تخلعي كل شيء
وتظلي كغابة من رخام
وأنا اليوم لا أريدك إلا
أن تكوني.. إشارة استفهام

50

وكلما انفصلتُ عن واحدة
أقول في سذاجة
سوف تكون المرأة الأخيرة
والمَرّة الأخيرة
وبعدها سقطْتُ في الغرام ألف مرة
ومتُّ ألف مرة
ولم أزل أقول
"تلك المرة الأخيرة"

51

عبثا ما أكتب سيدتي
إحساسي أكبر من لغتي
وشعوري نحوك يتخطى
صوتي.. يتخطى حنجرتي
عبثا ما أكتب.. ما دامت
كلماتي.. أوسع من شفتي
أكرهها كل كتاباتي
مشكلتي أنكِ مشكلتي

52

لأن حبي لك فوق مستوى الكلام
قررتُ أن أسكت.... والسلام

I Love You and the Rest to Come

Your conversation is a Persian rug
and your eyes are two Damascene birds
flying between two walls.
And my heart travels like a dove over the water of your hands
and takes a nap in the shadow of your bracelet
And I love you
but I fear getting entangled with you
uniting with you
morphing into you
I have learned to avoid loving women
and raging seas
I don't dispute your love; it is my morning
and I don't dispute the morning sun
I don't dispute your love
it decides when it is coming and what day it will leave
and it determines the narrative

Let me pour you some tea
You are fabulously beautiful this morning
and your voice is an engraving on a Moroccan dress
Your necklace dances under the mirrors like a child
then dips into the vase to sip water

Let me pour you some tea
Did I say that I love you
and that I am happy you're here
and that your presence pleases me like the presence of a poem
like the arrival of boats and distant memories

Let me translate for you the words of the chairs when they
   welcome you
Let me tell you about what goes into the cups' minds

أحبك والبقية تأتي

حديثك سجادةٌ فارسية
وعيناك عصفورتان دمشقيتان
تطيران بين الجدار وبين الجدار
وقلبي يسافر مثل الحمامة فوق مياه يديك،
ويأخذ قيلولةً تحت ظلّ السوار
وإني أحبك
لكن أخاف التورط فيك،
أخاف التوحُّد فيك،
أخاف التقمُّص فيك،
فقد علمتني التجارب أن أتجنب عشق النساء،
وموج البحار
أنا لا أناقش حبك.. فهو نهاري
ولست أناقش شمس النهار
أنا لا أناقش حبك
فهو يقرّر في أي يومٍ سيأتي.. وفي أي يومٍ سيذهب
وهو يحدّد وقت الحوار، وشكل الحوار

دعيني أصبُّ لك الشاي،
أنت خرافية الحسن هذا الصباح،
وصوتك نقشٌ جميلٌ على ثوب مراكشية
وعقدك يلعب كالطفل تحت المرايا
ويرتشف الماء من شفة المزهرية

دعيني أصبُّ لك الشاي، هل قلت إني أحبك؟
هل قلت إني سعيدٌ لأنك جئت
وأن حضورك يُسعِدُ مثل حضور القصيدة
ومثل حضور المراكب، والذكريات البعيدة

دعيني أترجم بعض كلام المقاعد وهي ترحب فيك
دعيني، أعبّر عما يدور ببال الفناجين،

as they think about your lips
and the minds of the spoons and the saucers
Let me add a new letter to the alphabet
Let me contradict myself a little
and combine- in love- barbarism and civilization

Do you like the tea?
Do you want some milk?
Or you're content, as always, with a cube of sugar
Me, I prefer your face without sugar

I repeat for the thousandth time; I love you
How can I explain the inexplicable?
How can I measure the space of my sorrow
My sorrow is like a child: it grows more handsome with time
Let me tell you in all the languages, the ones you know and don't know,
that I love you
Let me look for a vocabulary
as expansive as my longing for you
and for words that cover your breasts
with water, grass, and jasmine
Let me think for you
long for you
cry and laugh for you
and let me cancel the distance between reality and imagination

Let me call you with all the calling letters;
maybe if I sing your name, you will be born from my lips
Let me construct a nation of love
where you are the queen
and I am the most notorious lover
Let me lead a coup
to assert the governing of your eyes among people

وهي تفكّر في شفتيك
وبال الملاعق، والسكرية
دعيني أضيفك حرفاً جديداً
على أحرف الأبجدية
دعيني أناقض نفسي قليلاً
وأجْمَع في الحب بين الحضارة والبربرية

أأعجبك الشاي؟
هل ترغبين ببعض الحليب؟
وهل تكتفين – كما كنت دوماً – بقطعة سُكَّرٍ؟
وأما أنا فأفضّل وجهك من غير سُكَّرّ

أكرّر للمرة الألف أني أحبك
كيف تريدينني أن أفسِّر ما لا يُفسَّر؟
كيف تريدينني أن أقيس مساحة حزني؟
وحزني كالطفل.. يزداد في كل يوم جمالاً ويكبر
دعيني أقول بكل اللغات التي تعرفين والتي لا تعرفين
أحبك أنت
دعيني أُفتِّش عن مفرداتٍ
تكون بحجم حنيني إليك
وعن كلماتٍ.. تغطي مساحة نهديك
بالماء، والعشب، والياسمين
دعيني أفكر عنك
وأشتاق عنك
وأبكي، وأضحك عنك
وألغي المسافة بين الخيال وبين اليقين

دعيني أنادي عليك، بكل حروف النداء
لعلي إذا ما تغرغرت باسمك، من شفتيَّ تولدين
دعيني أؤسِّس دولة عشقٍ
تكونين أنت المليكة فيها
وأصبح فيها أنا أعظم العاشقين
دعيني أقود انقلاباً
يوطِّد سلطة عينيك بين الشعوب،

Let me, with love, change the face of civilization
You are the civilization. You are the heritage that formed from
　　within Earth
thousands of years ago

I love you
How do you want me to prove that your presence in the universe
is like the presence of water
and the presence of trees
And that you are a sunflower
and a field of palms
and a song that sailed from a string
Let me say you in silence
as sentences fail to express my anguish
as talking becomes an entangling conspiracy
and as the poem turns into a stone

Let me say you in between me and myself
and between my eyelashes and my eye
Let me say you in symbols if you don't trust the moonlight
let me say you in lightning
or rain drops
Let me—if you accept my invitation to travel—
the seas the address of your eyes

Why do I love you?
The boat does not remember how water came to surround it
does not remember how it suffered seasickness
Why do I love you?
The bullet in the flesh does not ask where it came from
and does not apologize
Why do I love you? Don't ask me
I don't have the choice, and neither do you

دعيني.. أغير بالحب وجه الحضارة
أنت الحضارة.. أنت التراث الذي يتشكل في باطن الأرض
منذ ألوف السنين

أحبك
كيف تريديني أن أبرهن أن حضورك في الكون،
مِثْل حضور المياه،
ومِثْل حضور الشجر
وأنك زهرة دوار شمسٍ
وبستان نخلٍ
وأغنيةٌ أبحرَت من وتر
دعيني أقولك بالصمت
حين تضيق العبارة عما أعاني
وحين يصير الكلام مؤامرةً أتورط فيها
وتغدو القصيدة آنيةً من حجر

دعيني
أقولك ما بين نفسي وبيني
وما بين أهداب عيني، وعيني
دعيني
أقولك بالرمز، إن كنت لا تثقين بضوء القمر
دعيني أقولك بالبرق،
أو برذاذ المطر
دعيني أُقدّم للبحر عنوان عينيك
إن تَقبَّلي دعوتي للسفر
لماذا أحبك؟

إن السفينة في البحر، لا تتذكر كيف أحاط بها الماء
لا تتذكر كيف اعتراها الدوار
لماذا أحبك؟
إن الرصاصة في اللحم لا تتساءل من أين جاءت
وليست تُقدِّم أي اعتذار
لماذا أحبك.. لا تسأليني
فليس لدي الخيار... وليس لديك الخيار

Squares

1

I am a square
Looking— since the first century—
for the rest of its sides
looking since the beginning of existence
for a picture of its face
looking— since the starting of days—
for its lost woman

2

I am Jesus, the son of Mary
looking for the history of my crucifixion
for my blood, my wounds, and my nails

3

I am in a square; its name is you
I can't escape it to another woman
I am bound tightly between your breasts
I can't escape that abyss even if I want to

4

I am in a square called poetry
I can't go north
I can't go south
and I know that I am going to be killed
by a knockout

5

I am an Arabic poet who dies
on the dagger of love one day
and on the dagger of the alphabet on another

مُرَّبعات

1

أنا مربعٌ
يبحث منذ القرن الأول
عن بقية أضلاعه
يبحث منذ بدايات التكوين
عن صورة وجهه
يبحث منذ بدايات النساء
عن اسم امرأته الضائعة

2

أنا المسيح عيسى بن مريم
أبحث منذ تاريخ صلبي
عن دمي... وجراحي... ومساميري

3

أنا في مربَّع، اسمه أنتِ
فلا أستطيع الهروب إلى امرأةٍ ثانية
أنا بين نهديك في مأزقٍ
ولا أستطيع الخلاص من الهاوية

4

أنا في مربَّع اسمه الشعر
فلا أستطيع الذهاب شمالاً
ولا أستطيع الذهاب جنوباً
وأعرف أنّي سأُقتَلُ بالضربة القاضية

5

أنا شاعرٌ عربي... يموت
على خنجر العشق يوماً
ويوماً... على خنجر القافية

6

I am in a square called femininity
What beauty will set me free
if there are no *Lubnah* and no *Raweea*?

7

I am in a square called Poem
she wears me as a bracelet
she imprisons me in her rings
she besieges me in her braids
she wraps me around her feet like an anklet

8

I am in a square opened to you
from the four sides
from the black hair to the silver earrings
and from the fingers studded with stars
to the countless freckles

9

I am a green square in the sea of your eyes
I am still sailing
I am still drowning
I am still floating and mooring
And I don't know, my precious, when
I would arrive at the sand of your chest

10

I am in a square called writing
and I can't free myself from you
I can't free myself from me
Where are your hands
to light up my future days

6

أنا في مربّعٍ اسمه الأنوثة
فأي الجميلات تُفرجُ عني
وليس هنالك أبَنَى... ولا راوية

7

أنا في مربّعٍ... اسمه القصيدة
في أساورها تلبسني
في خواتمها تحبسني
في ضفائرها تحاصرني
في قدميها تزيّن بي
كخلاخيل الحرية

8

أنا في مربّعٍ مفتوحٍ عليك
من الجهات الأربع
من الشعر الأسود... إلى الحَلَق الفضيّ
ومن الأصابع المرصعة بالنجوم
الى الشامات التي لا عدد لها

9

أنا مربّعٌ أخضر... في بحر عينيك
وما زلت أبحر
ما زلت اغرق
ما زلت أطفو... وأرسو
وأجهل في أي وقت
يكون وصولي
الى رمل صدرك... أيتها الغالية

10

أنا في مربّعٍ... اسمه الكتابة
ولا أستطيع التحرر منك
ولا أستطيع التحرر مني
فأين يداك
تضيعان أيامي الآتية

11

I love you
O the one that I collect the remaining of my dreams
from her lips

12

I love you
O the thousand women in my clothes
O the thousand verses of poetry
that fill my papers.

Lubnah Bint Al-Habab: Lubnah lived in the seventh century AD. She was a poet, but famously known for her love story with Qays Ibn Dhurayh, a poet who wrote volumes of poetry in her honor.

Raweea: We believe might be a reference to Scheherazade, the narrator of the Arabic collection of tales known as *One Thousand and One Nights*.

11
أحبكِ
يا مَن ألملم من شفتيها
بقية أحلامي الباقية

12
أحبكِ
يا ألف امرأةٍ في ثيابي
ويا ألف بيتٍ من الشِعر
يملأُ أوراقي

Painting with Words

Don't ask me about my life's story
it is long, my queen, so long
I have existed in all centuries
as if I were a million-year-old
My luggage is worn out from the long travels
My horse is tired to the bone from my excursions
There is no breast black or white
that I didn't plant my flag on its ground
that I didn't pass over with my wagons
I wore women's skin like an abaya
I built pyramids from their nipples
I wrote poetry; its magic has no match
except for God's words in the ancient Torah

Today I sit on my ship
like a thief looking for a way out
I turn the key to the women's room
I only see skulls in the shadow
Where are the concubines I owned?
Where is the incense lost from my chamber?
Today the breasts avenge themselves
and return my stabbing with stabs

The tragedy of *Haroun Al-Rashid* is painful
but if you only knew how painful mine is
I am like a street lamp, my lady
I cry, and no one sees my tears
Sex was a home I tried
but it didn't end my problems or my sorrows
And all love became the same
like the forest leaves
I now can't love an ant

الرسم بالكلمات

لا تطلبي مني حساب حياتي
إن الحديث يطول يا مولاتي
كل العصور أنا بها.. فكأنما
عمري ملايينٌ من السنوات
تَعِبَتْ من السفر الطويل حقائبي
وتَعِبْتُ من خيلي ومن غزواتي
لم يبقى نهدٌ.. أسودٌ أو أبيضٌ
إلا زَرَعتُ بأرضه راياتي
إلا ومرّت فوقها عرباتي
فصَّلْتُ من جلد النساء عباءةً
وبنيتُ أهراماً من الحلمات
وكتبتُ شعراً.. لا يشابه سحره
إلا كلام الله في التَّوراة

واليوم أجلس فوق سطح سفينتي
كاللَّص.. أبحثُ عن طريق نجاة
وأديرُ مفتاح الحريم.. فلا أرى
في الظلّ غير جماجم الأموات
أين السبايا.. أين ملَّكَتْ يدي؟
أين البخور يضوع من حجراتي؟
اليوم تنتقم النهود لنفسها
وتردُّ لي الطعنات بالطعنات

مأساة هارون الرشيد مريرة
لو تدركين مرارة المأساة
إني كمصباح الطريق.. صديقتي
أبكي.. ولا أحد يرى دمعاتي
الجنس كان مُسَكِّناً جرّبتُهُ
لم يُنهي أحزاني ولا أزماتي
والحب أصبح كلّهُ متشابهاً
كتشابه الأوراق في الغابات
أنا عاجزٌ عن عشق أية نملة

or a cloud or a pebble
I tried thousands of things to believe in, and I found
it is best to believe in me

Your sweet mouth doesn't resolve my predicament;
my predicament is in my notebooks and my ink
All roads ahead are closed
and our deliverance is in painting with words

Haroun Al-Rashid (763-809 AD): the fifth Abbasid caliph (786-809 AD), ruled over the Golden Age of Islam and saw its decline into division. He is known for his relentless pursuit of women and pleasure. He kept many mistresses in the women's court in his palaces at his disposal.

أو غيمةٍ.. عن عشق أي حصاة
مارستُ ألف عبادةٍ وعبادةٍ
فوجدتُ أفضلها عبادة ذاتي

فمك المطيّبُ.. لا يحلُّ قضيّتي
فقضيّتي في دفتري ودواتي
كل الدروب أمامنا مسدودةٌ
وخلاصنا.. في الرسم بالكلمات

The Trial

The Middle East embraces my poems and condemns them
A thousand thanks to those who endorsed them
and a thousand more to those who cursed them
For I defended the blood of slain women
I backed their breasts' revolution
and I gave to each terrified one of them
a country
I did not hesitate to pay the price
I am with love, even if I have to die for it
If I abandon my passion, I won't be who I am

المحاكمة

يعانق الشرق أشعاري.. ويلعنها
فألف شكرٍ لمن أطرى.. ومن لعنا
فكم مذبوحة.. دافعت عن دمها
كل خائفة أهديتها وطناً
وكل نهد.. أنا أيّدت ثورته
وما ترددتُ في أن أدفع الثمن
أنا مع الحب حتى حين يقتلني
إذا تخليت عن عشقي.. فلست أنا

Standing in Lines

I asked for some sunshine
The policeman said,
Stand in line, mister
I asked for some ink to write my name
They said,
Ink is scarce
Stand in line
I asked for a book to read
The man in the military uniform screamed,
If you want education, you should read the party's propaganda
and the constitution
I asked for permission to meet my woman
They answered,
Meeting women is difficult, and lovers
should not get frustrated with standing in line
I asked for permission to have a child
The general said, laughing
Having kids is important
Stand in line for another year
I asked to see the face of God
One of the religious men screamed,
Why?
I said,
Because I am oppressed
So he pointed with his finger
and I understood that there was a line for the oppressed too
God, I wish to meet you
don't leave me like a stray dog standing in line
Since I came to this world
I have been planted, standing in lines
My legs are frozen in the snow
My soul is scattered leaves

الطابور

طالبت ببعض الشمس،
قال رجال الشرطة:
قِفْ – يا سيد – في الطابور
طالبت ببعض الحبر، لأكتب اسمي
قالوا: إن الحبر قليلٌ
فالزَمْ دورك في الطابور
طالبتُ بأي كتاب أقرأ فيه
فصاح قميصٌ كاكيٌّ
من كان يريد العلم
فإن عليه، قراءة منشورات الحزب
وأحكام الدستور
طالبتُ بإذنٍ حتى ألقى امرأتي
فأجابوني: إن لقاء المرأة صعبٌ
وعلى العاشق،
أن لاييأس من طول الطابور
طالبتُ بإذنٍ
حتى أنجب ولداً
قال نقيبٌ، وهو يقهقه
إن النسل مهمٌّ جدا
فلتنتظر، سنةً أخرى، في الطابور
طالبتُ برؤية وجه الله
فصاح وكيلٌ من وكلاء الله
(لماذا؟)
قلت: لأني إنسانٌ مقهور
فأشار إليَّ بإصبعه
وفهمتُ بأن المقهورين
لهم أيضاً طابور...
أرجو أن ألقاك.. ولكن لا تتركني
مثل كلاب الشارع، في الطابور
من يوم أتيتُ إلى الدنيا
وأنا مزروعٌ في الطابور
ساقاي تجمدتا في الثلج،
ونفسي كالورق المنثور

waiting for a homeland that doesn't come
and for a warm seaside and birds
I don't know how to recite poetry
For every place I go, a machete follows me
All the papers are booby-trapped
All the pencils are booby-trapped
All the breasts are booby-trapped
And the bed of love
requires a passport
God,
this nation is crouching between water and water
sad like a broken sword
If we say goodbye to camphor
more camphor arrives to dull our resolve
God,
this horizon is gray
If you want to help me, turn me into a bird
I long for a spot of light
God, if you want to help me
turn me into a bird

منتظرٌ وطناً.. لا يأتي
وشواطئ دافئةً.. وطيور
لا أدري.. كيف أقول الشعر
فحيث ذهبتُ يلاحقني الساطور
كل الأوراق مفخخةٌ
كل الأقلام مفخخةٌ
كل الأثداء مفخخةٌ
وسرير الحب
يريد جواز مرور
يا ربي:
وهذا الوطن القابع بين الماء.. وبين الماء
حزينٌ كالسيف المكسور
فإذا ودَّعنا كافوراً
يأتينا.. أكثر من كافور
يا ربي
إن الأفق رماديّ
إن كنت تريد مساعدتي
يا ربي.. فاجعلني عصفور
وأنا أشتاق لقطرة نور
إن كنت تريد مساعدتي
يا ربي.. فاجعلني عصفور

The Train of Sorrows

I take thousands of trains
and I ride my tragedy
I ride the smoke of my cigarette
In my one luggage,
I carry the addresses of my lovers
and those of my ex lovers
The train runs fast, fast
and chews up the flesh of distances on its way
devours the orchids on its way
devours the trees on its way
and licks the feet of lakes
The train's conductor asks me about my ticket
and my next stop—
is there another stop?
The hotels of the world don't know me
or the addresses of my lovers
There is no sidewalk I go to on my trips
My sidewalks are all running away from me
My sidewalks are all running away from me

قطار الأحزان

أركب آلاف القطارات
وأمتطي فجيعتي
وأمتطي غيم سجاراتي
حقيبة واحدة.. أحملها
فيها عناوين حبيباتي
من كُنَّ، بالأمس، حبيباتي
يمضي قطاري مسرعاً.. مسرعاً
يمضغ في طريقه لحم المسافات
يفترس الحقول في طريقه
يلتهم الأشجار في طريقه
يلحس أقدام البحيرات
يسألني مفتش القطار عن تذكرتي
وموقفي الآتي
وهل هناك موقف آتي؟
فنادق العالم لا تعرفني
ولا عناوين حبيباتي
لا رصيف لي
أقصده.. في كل رحلاتي
أرصفتي جميعها.. هاربة
هاربة.. مني محطاتي
هاربة.. مني محطاتي

Bread, Hashish, and the Moon

When the moon is born in the East
the white roofs sleep under layers of flowers
People leave their shops and go in groups
to meet it

They carry bread and a radio and opium to the mountaintop
They buy and sell fantasies
and visions
bewitched by the moon
wasted to death if the moon lives

What does a disc of light do to my country
the country of the prophets
and of the gullible who chew tobacco and deal in a stupor?
What does the moon do that we surrender our pride
and beg the sky to save us?
What does the sky have for the lazy and weak
wasted to death in the witching moon
those who shake the prophets' tombs for rice and children
the tombs of Awliyaa
where they spread their embellished rugs
and amuse themselves with the opium of destiny and fate
in my nation, a nation of the gullible?

خبز وحشيش وقمر

عندما يولدُ في الشرق القمر
فالسطوح البيض تغفو
تحت أكداس الزهر
يترك الناس الحوانيت ويمضون زُمَر
لملاقاة القمر

يحملون الخبز.. والحاكي.. إلى رأس الجبال
ومعدات الخدر
ويبيعون.. ويشترون.. خيَال
وصور
ويموتون إذا عاش القمر

ما الذي يفعله قرص ضياء؟
ببلادي
ببلاد الأنبياء
وبلاد البسطاء
ماضغي التبغ وتجَّار الخدر
ما الذي يفعله فينا القمر؟
فنُضيّع الكبرياء
ونعيش لنستجدي السماء
ما الذي عند السماء
لِكسالى.. ضعفاء؟
يسلخيلون إلى موتى إذا عاش القمر
ويهزُّون قبور الأولياء
علّها ترززقهم رزاً.. وأطفالاً.. قبور الأولياء
ويمدّون السجاجيد الأنيقات الطرر
يتسلون بأفيون نسميه قدر
وقضاء
في بلادي.. في بلاد البسطاء

What weakness and decay
come upon us when the light flows?
The rugs and thousands of chains
and teacups and children occupy the hills
in my country
where the people cry for a light they can't see
where people live without eyes
where the simple people cry and pray and sin
and on their mystical hoodoo
live dependent

They call "O crescent moon
O the spring that rains diamonds
and hashish and drowsiness
O marble God
O Unbelievable
May you live for the East, for us
like a cluster of diamonds
for the millions who have lost their wits
and their way"

On Middle Eastern nights
when the moon is full
the Middle East sheds its dignity
and its will to toil
The millions who run without shoes
and believe in four wives
and the day of judgment
The millions who find bread
only in dreams
and live at night in houses loud with coughing

أي ضعف وانحلال
يتولانا إذا الضوء تدفق
فالسجاجيد.. وآلاف السلال
وقداح الشاي.. والأطفال.. تحتل التلال
في بلادي
حيث يبكي الساذجون
ويعيشون على الضوء الذي لا يبصرون
في بلادي
حيث يحيا الناس من دون عيون
حيث يبكي الساذجون
ويصلون
ويزنون
ويحيون اتكال
منذ أن كانوا يعيشون اتكال

وينادون الهلال
"يا هلال
أيها النبع الذي يمطر ماس
وحشيشياً.. ونعاس
أيها الرب الرخامي المعلّق
أيها الشيء الذي ليس يُصدّق
دمت للشرق.. لنا
عنقود ماس
للملايين التي عطّلَت فيها الحواس"

في ليالي الشرق لمّا
يبلغ البدر تمامه
يتعرّى الشرق من كل كرامة
ونضال
فالملايين التي تركض من غير نعال
والتي تؤمن في أربع زوجاتٍ
وفي يوم القيامة
الملايين التي لا تلتقي بالخبز
إلا في الخيال
والتي تسكن في الليل بيوتاً من سعال

—they've never known what medicine is
Their bodies fall like corpses to rot under the light
in my country where the gullible cry
and die of crying when the crescent moon rises
and cry more when they listen to the oud
and the songs drawn out for hours
—that death we call in the Middle East *Liali*
In my country
the country of simple people
we mull over long songs
—a tuberculosis that kills us—
the long songs
Our Middle East that dwells on history
and idle dreams and old fables
still looks for heroism in *Abu Zeid Al-Hilali*
our legend from the eleventh century

This poem angered religious leaders in Syria in 1955. They requested that Parliament convene and discuss some punishment. That was the first time that a poem had to be discussed in Parliament. They decided not to let Qabbani publish the poem. Instead, Qabbani went to London and published it there.

Liali: It refers to the nights when people gathered in restaurants to drink, smoke, eat, and listen to long songs for hours (like Oum Kalthoum songs), sometimes until dawn. Here, Qabbani emphasizes the plague of a culture that spends its time on nonproductive activities.

Abu Zeid Al-Hilali: He was an eleventh-century leader who grew to be a legendary hero. When some tribes in Tunisia adopted Sunniism, the Ismaili Caliph sent Abu Zeid to fight them. He traveled with his tribe, Banou Hilali, from what is now Iraq and Syria to Tunisia through Egypt; He fought a vicious war and won. He became a legend because, over time, people confabulated more heroic imaginary fables around his name. Here, the poet invokes the hero to say that the Middle East cannot create new heroes; thus, it always returns to its ancient heroes to claim heroism.

أبدأ.. ما عرفتُ شكل الدواء
تترَدَّى جثثاً تحت الضياء
في بلادي.. حيث يبكي الأغبياء
ويموتون بكاء
كلما حرَّكَهم عودٌ ذليلٌ.. و"ليالي"
ذلك الموت الذي ندعوه في الشرق
"ليالي".. وغناء
في بلادي
في بلاد البسطاء
حيث نجتَّر التواشيح الطويلة
ذلك السلُّ الذي يفتك بالشرق
التواشيح الطويلة

شرقنا المجتَّر.. تاريخاً
وأحلاماً كسولة
وخرافاتٍ خوالي
شرقنا الباحث عن كل بطولة
في أبي زيد الهلالي

A Lesson in Drawing

1

My son places his coloring kit in front of me
and asks me to draw a bird
I dip the brush in the color gray
and I draw a square with a lock
and rods
My son asks with wonder in his eyes,
"Dad, don't you know how to draw a bird?"
I say, "Forgive me, son,
I have forgotten the shape of birds"

2

My son places his coloring pencils in front of me
and asks me to draw the sea
I take a pencil,
and I draw a black circle
My son says,
"But this is a black circle, Dad!
Don't you know the sea is blue?"
I say,
"My son, I used to be good at drawing seas
but they took away my fishing rod and my boat
They prohibited me from conversing with the color blue
and from fishing in the waters of freedom"

3

My son places his drawing notebook in front of me
and asks me to draw a stalk of wheat
I hold a pencil,
and I draw a gun

درس في الرسم

1

يضع إبني ألوانه أمامي
ويطلب مني أن أرسم له عصفوراً
أغطُّ الفرشاة باللون الرمادي
وأرسم له مربعاً عليه قفلٌ.. وقضبان
يقول لي إبني، والدهشة تملأ عينيه
.. ولكن هذا سجنٌ
ألا تعرف، يا أبي، كيف ترسم عصفوراً؟؟
أقول له: يا ولدي.. لا تؤاخذني
فقد نسيتُ شكل العصافير

2

يضع إبني علبة أقلامه أمامي
ويطلب مني أن أرسم له بحراً
آخذ قلم الرصاص،
وأرسم له دائرةً سوداء
يقول لي إبني
ولكن هذه دائرةٌ سوداء، يا أبي
ألا تعرف أن ترسم بحراً؟
ثم ألا تعرف أن لون البحر أزرق
أقول له: يا ولدي
كنت في زماني شاطراً في رسم البحار
أما اليوم.. فقد أخذوا مني الصنّارة
وقارب الصيد
ومنعوني من الحوار مع اللون الأزرق
واصطياد سمك الحرية

3

يضع إبني كراسة الرسم أمامي
ويطلب مني أن أرسم له سنبلة قمح
أمسك القلم
وأرسم له مسدساً

My son mocks my ignorance of the art of drawing
and says, wondering,
"Don't you know, Dad, the difference between a stalk of wheat and
   a gun?"
I say, "My son, in the past, I used to know the shape of wheat stalks
and the shape of a loaf of bread
and the shape of a flower,
but in this iron world
where the forest's trees join militias
and the roses wear camouflage;
in this time of the armed ears of corn
and armed birds
and armed religion,
I can't buy a loaf of bread
without finding a gun hidden inside it
I can't pluck a flower from the field
without it raising a weapon in my face
No book I buy from the library
doesn't explode between my fingers"

4

My son sits on the edge of the bed
and asks me to read him a poem
One tear drops from my eyes on the pillow;
he catches it in astonishment and says,
"But this is a tear and not a poem, dad!"
I say,
"When you grow up, my son,
and read the volumes of Arabic poetry,
you will know that the word and the tear are sisters
and that the Arabic poem
is but a tear shed from the tips of the fingers"

يسخر إبني من جهلي في فنّ الرسم
ويقول مستغرباً
ألا تعرف يا أبي الفرق بين السنبلة.. والمسدس؟
أقول يا ولدي
كنت أعرف في الماضي شكل السنبلة
وشكل الرغيف
وشكل الوردة
أما في هذا الزمن المعدني
الذي انضمت فيه أشجار الغابة
إلى رجال الميليشيات
وأصبحتُ فيه الوردة تلبس الملابس المرقطة
في زمن السنابل المسلحة
والعصافير المسلحة
والديانة المسلحة
فلا رغيف أشتريه
إلا وأجد في داخله مسدساً
ولا وردة أقطفها من الحقل
إلا وترفع سلاحها في وجهي
ولا كتاب أشتريه من المكتبة
إلا وينفجر بين أصابعي

4

يجلس إبني على طرف سريري
ويطلب منيّ أنْ أسمعه قصيدة
تسقط مني دمعةٌ على الوسادة
فيلتقطها مذهولاً.. ويقول
ولكن هذه دمعةٌ، يا أبي، وليست قصيدة
أقول له
عندما تكبُر يا ولدي
وتقرأ ديوان الشعر العرب
سوف تَعرفُ أن الكلمة والدمعة شقيقتان
وأن القصيدة العربية
ليست سوى دمعة تخرج من بين الأصابع

5
My son places his coloring pencils and coloring kits in front of me
and asks me to draw a country
The brush shakes in my hand
and I fall crying

5

يضع إبني أقلامه، وعلبة ألوانه أمامي
ويطلب مني أن أرسم له وطناً
تهتز الفرشاة في يدي
وأسقط باكياً

Balqis

Thank you
Thank you
The woman I love was murdered
Now, you can have a drink at the martyr's grave
My poem was assassinated
Would any nation on Earth except us
assassinate a poem?

Balqis
was the most beautiful queen in the history of Babylon
Balqis
was the tallest palm in the land of Iraq
When she walked,
peacocks joined her
and gazelles followed her

Balqis,
O my pain
and the pain of the poem when I touch it
After your hair, would the wheat stalks grow?
O my green *Nineveh*
O my blonde gypsy
O the waves of the Tigris—
anklets on feet as springtime arrives
They killed you, Balqis
What kind of a nation
assassinates the Bulbuls' voices
Where are the *Al-Samaw'al*
and the *Al-Muhalhil*
and the first noble men?

بلقيس

شكراً لكم
شكراً لكم
فحبيبتي قُتِلت.. وصار بوسعكم
أن تشربوا كأساً على قبر الشهيدة
وقصيدتي أغتيلَت
وهل من أمةٍ في الأرض
إلا نحن - تغتال القصيدة؟

بلقيس
كانت أجمل الملكات في تاريخ بابل
بلقيس
كانت أطول النخلات في أرض العراق
كانت إذا تمشي
ترافقها طواويسٌ
وتتبعها أيائل

بلقيس.. يا وجعي
ويا وجع القصيدة حين تلمسها الأنامل
هل يا تُرى
من بَعدِ شعرك سوف ترتفع السنابل؟
يا نينوى الخضراء
يا غجريتي الشقراء
يا أمواج دجلة
تَلبس في الربيع بساقها
أحلى الخلاخل
قتلوك يا بلقيس
أية أمةٍ عربيةٍ
تلك التي
تغتال أصوات البلابل؟
أين السموأل؟
والمهلهل؟
والغطاريف الأوائل؟

Tribes ate tribes
and wolves killed wolves
and spiders killed spiders
I swear to your eyes
to which millions of stars migrate
I will say, O my moon, wondrous tales about the Arabs
Is heroism an Arabic lie?
Or, like us, our history is a lie?

Balqis,
Don't disappear
The sun after you
won't shine on the coasts
I will say during the interrogation
that the thief wears a hero's uniform
and the talented leader is a contractor
I will say that the nuclear bomb is nothing
but a sick joke
We are a tribe among tribes
This is our history, Balqis
How can one tell gardens from garbage

Balqis,
O the martyr and the poem
Sheba is looking for its queen;
return the people's greetings
O the most glorious queen
O woman who embodies all the Sumerian glories

Balqis,
O my most beautiful bird
O my most precious icon
O the tears that fell on Mary Magdalen's cheeks

فقبائلُ أكَلَت قبائل
وثعالبٌ قَتَلَت ثعالب
وعناكبٌ قَتَّلَت عناكب
قسماً بعينيك اللتين إليهما
تأوي ملايين الكواكب
سأقول، يا قمري، عن العرب العجائب
فهل البطولة كذبةٌ عربيةٌ؟
أم مِثلُنا التاريخ كاذب؟

بلقيس
لا تتغيبي عني
فإن الشمس بعدك
لا تضيء على السواحل
سأقول في التحقيق
إن اللِصَّ أصبَحَ يرتدي ثوب المقاتل
وأقول في التحقيق
إن القائد الموهوب أصبَحَ كالمقاول
وأقول
إن حكاية الإشعاع، أسخف نكتةٍ قيلْت
فنحن قبيلةٌ بين القبائل
هذا هو التاريخ.. يا بلقيس
كيف يُفَرِّق الإنسان
ما بين الحدائق والمزابل

بلقيس
أيتها الشهيدة.. والقصيدة
والمطَهَّرة النقية
سبأ تُفَتِّش عن مليكتها
فرِدِّي للجماهير التحية
يا أعظم الملكات
يا امرأةً تجسِّد كل أمجاد العصور السومرية

بلقيس
يا عصفورتي الأحلى
ويا أيقونتي الأغلى
ويا دمعاً تناثر فوق خدِّ المجدَّلية

Was it an injustice moving you from the *A'azamiah's* banks?

Beirut kills one of us every day;
it searches for a victim daily
Death is in the cup of coffee
in our apartment's key
in the flowers on the balcony
in the newspapers' leaflets
in our alphabet
Here we are, Balqis,
entering medieval time
Here we are, entering savagery
backwardness, ugliness, and despicability;
entering, once again, barbarity
where writing is a trip between one bullet and the next
where killing a butterfly in the field became the case at hand

Do you know Balqis, the woman I love?
She was the most valuable verse in the books of love
She was a wonderful mix
of marigold and marble
Between her eyes
violets slept and woke up

Balqis,
You are the fragrance in my memory
You are a tomb that traveled to the clouds
They killed you in Beirut, like any gazelle
And after you, they killed all the words

Balqis,
This is not a requiem;
it is a farewell to the Arabs

أترى ظلمتُكِ إذ نقلتُكِ
ذات يومٍ.. من ضفاف الأعظمية

بيروت.. تَقْتُل كل يوم واحداً منا
وتبحث كل يوم عن ضحية
والموت.. في فنجان قهوتنا
وفي مفتاح شقتنا
وفي أزهار شرفتنا
وفي ورق الجرائد
والحروف الأبجدية
ها نحن.. يا بلقيس
ندخل مرةً أخرى لعصر الجاهلية
ها نحن ندخل في التوحُّش
والتخلُّف.. والبشاعة.. والوضاعة
ندخل مرةً أخرى.. عصور البربرية
حيث الكتابة رحلةٌ
بين الشظيَّة.. والشظيَّة
حيث اغتيال فراشةٍ في حقلها
صار القضية

هل تعرفون حبيبتي بلقيس؟
فهي أهمُّ ما كتبوه في كتب الغرام
كانت مزيجاً رائعاً
بين القطيفة والرخام
كان البنفسج بين عينيها
ينام ولا ينام

بلقيس
يا عطراً بذاكرتي
ويا قبراً يسافر في الغمام
قتلوك، في بيروت، مِثل أي غزالةٍ
من بعدما.. قتلوا الكلام

بلقيس
ليست هذه مرثية
لكن
على العرب السلام

Balqis,
We are yearning, yearning, yearning
The small house looks for its princess' perfumed footsteps
We listen to the news
and the news is ambiguous and ambivalent

Balqis,
We are slaughtered to the bone
The children don't know what is happening
and I don't know what to say
Are you going to knock on the door in a few minutes?
Are you going to take off your winter coat?
Are you going to come smiling and lively
and shine like the field's flowers?

Balqis,
Your green plants
still on the walls, crying
and your face still moves
between the mirrors and the curtains
Even the cigarette you lit
is not yet extinguished
and its fume refuses to leave

Balqis,
We are stabbed, stabbed to the bone
and astonishment lives in our eyes

Balqis,
how did you take my days and dreams
how did you cancel all gardens and all seasons?

بلقيس
مشتاقون.. مشتاقون.. مشتاقون
والبيت الصغير
يسائل عن أميرته المعطَّرة الذيول
نُصغي إلى الأخبار.. والأخبار غامضةٌ
ولا تروي فضول

بلقيس
مذبوحون حتى العَظْم
والأولاد لا يدرون ما يجري
ولا أدري أنا.. ماذا أقول؟
هل تقرعين الباب بعد دقائق؟
هل تخلعين المعطف الشتوي؟
هل تأتين باسمةً
وناضرةً
ومشرقةً كأزهار الحقول؟

بلقيس
إنَّ زروعك الخضراء
ما زالت على الحيطان باكيةً
ووجهك لم يزل متنقلاً
بين المرايا والستائر
حتى سجارتك التي أشعلتِها
لم تنطفئ
ودخانها
ما زال يرفض أن يسافر

بلقيس
مطعونون.. مطعونون في الأعماق
والأحداق يسكنها الذهول

بلقيس
كيف أخذتِ أيامي.. وأحلامي
وألغيتِ الحدائق والفصول

My wife,
my love, my friend, my poem, the light of my eyes,
my most beautiful bird,
how did you, Balqis, fly away from me?

Balqis,
It is time for the Iraqi, flavorful tea,
vintage like the best of wine
But who is going to pass the cups around, O my giraffe
who brought to our house the Euphrates
and the flowers of the Tigris and *Al-Rusafa*?

Balqis,
Sorrow pierces me
And Beirut who killed you does not recognize its crime
And Beirut who adored you
doesn't know that she killed her lover
and turned off the moon

Balqis,
O Balqis,
O Balqis,
Each cloud is mourning you;
who is going to mourn me?
Balqis, how did you leave in silence
without holding my hand?
Balqis,
How did you leave us in the wind
shivering like leaves?
And left –the three of us– lost
like feathers in the rain?
Didn't you think of me?
I need your love, just like *Zeinab and Omar*

يا زوجتي
وحبيبتي.. وقصيدتي.. وضياء عيني
قد كنتِ عصفوري الجميل
فكيف هربتِ يا بلقيس مني؟

بلقيس
هذا موعد الشاي العراقي المعطَّر
والمعتَّق كالسلافة
فمن الذي سيوزع الأقداح.. أيتها الزرافة؟
ومن الذي نَقَلَ الفرات لبيتنا
وورود دجلة والرصافة؟

بلقيس
إن الحزن يثقبني
وبيروت التي قتلتكِ.. لا تدري جريمتها
وبيروت التي عشقتكِ
تجهل أنها قتلت عشيقتها
وأطفأت القمر

بلقيس
يا بلقيس
يا بلقيس
كل غمامةٍ تبكي عليك
فمن ترى يبكي عليَّ
بلقيس.. كيف رَحَلْتِ صامتةً
ولم تضعي يديكِ.. على يديا؟
بلقيس
كيف تركتِنا في الريح
نَرْجُفْ مثل أوراق الشجر؟
وتركتِنا – نحن الثلاثة – ضائعين
كريشةٍ تحت المطر
أتراك ما فكرت بي؟
وأنا الذي يحتاج حبك.. مثل (زينب) أو (عمر)

Balqis,
O the magical treasure
O the Iraqi arrow
O the bamboo forest
O you who challenged the stars with pride
How did you conjure all that vigor?

Balqis,
the friend, the partner,
the tender like tulips,
Beirut is closing on us
the sea is closing on us
the place is closing on us

Balqis,
You can't be repeated—
there are no two of you

Balqis,
The little details of our relationships slaughter me
and the minutes and the seconds whip me
For, to each small pin, there is a story
and to each necklace of yours, there are two stories
Even the bobby pins of your golden hair
drench me as usual with the rain of tenderness
The beautiful Iraqi voice climbs
over the curtains
and the seats
and the plates
and you emerge from the mirrors
from the rings, you emerge
from the poem, you emerge
from the candles
from the red wine glasses

بلقيس
يا كنزاً خرافياً
ويا رمحاً عراقياً
وغابة خيزران
يا من تحَدّيت النجوم ترفعاً
من أين جئت بكل هذا العنفوان؟

بلقيس
أيتها الصديقة.. والرفيقة
والرقيقة مثل زهرة أقحوان
ضاقت بنا بيروت.. ضاق البحر
ضاق بنا المكان

بلقيس: ما أنت التي تتكررين
فما لبلقيس اثنتان

بلقيس
تذبحني التفاصيل الصغيرة في علاقتنا
وتجلدني الدقائق والثواني
فلكل دبوسٍ صغيرٍ قصة
ولكل عقدٍ من عقودك قصتان
حتى ملاقط شعرك الذهبي
تغمرني، كعادتها، بأمطار الحنان
ويُعرّش الصوت العراقي الجميل
على الستائر
والمقاعد
والأواني
ومن المرايا تطلعين
من الخواتم تطلعين
من القصيدة تطلعين
من الشموع
من الكؤوس
من النبيذ الأرجواني

Balqis,
O Balqis, O Balqis,
I wish you knew about the pain of the space
In each corner, you hover like a bird
There, you were smoking
There, you were reading
There, you were combing your hair like a palm tree
And there, you entered to greet the guests
like a Yemeni sword

Balqis,
Where are the perfume bottles
and the blue lighter?
Where is the Kent cigarette that never left your lips?
Where are the celebratory songs of your presence?
The combs remember their past and cry
they are longing for you too
Balqis,
It is difficult to migrate from my own blood
And I am besieged between the flames of fire
and the flames of the fumes

Balqis, O the princess,
You are burning in a war between one tribe and another
What do I write about the death of my queen?
Words are my scandal
Here we are, looking in the mound of victims
for a fallen star
for a body that shattered like mirrors
Here we are, asking
if this is your grave
or the grave of Arabism

بلقيس
يا بلقيس.. يا بلقيس
لو تدرين ما وجع المكان
في كل ركنٍ.. أنت حائمةٌ كعصفورٍ
وعابقةٌ كغابة بيلسان
فهناك.. كنت تدخنين
هناك.. كنت تطالعين
هناك.. كنت كنخلةٍ تتمشطين
وتدخلين على الضيوف
كأنك السيف اليمني

بلقيس
أين زجاجة (الغيرلان)؟
والولاعة الزرقاء
أين سجارة الـ (الكنت) التي
ما فارقت شفتيك؟
أين (الهاشمي) مغنياً
فوق القوام المهرجان
تتذكر الأمشاط ماضيها
فيكُرُج دمعها
هل يا ترى الأمشاط من أشواقها أيضاً تعاني؟
بلقيس: صعبٌ أن أهاجر من دمي
وأنا المحاصر بين ألسنة اللهيب
وبين ألسنة الدخان

بلقيس: أيتها الأميرة
ها أنت تحترقين.. في حرب العشيرة والعشيرة
ماذا سأكتب عن رحيل مليكتي؟
إن الكلام فضيحتي
ها نحن نبحث بين أكوام الضحايا
عن نجمةٍ سقطَت
وعن جسدٍ تناثر كالمرايا
ها نحن نسأل يا حبيبة
إن كان هذا القبر قبرك أنت
أم قبر العروبة

Balqis,
O the willow that dangled her braid over me
O the proud like a giraffe
Balqis,
Our Arabic destiny is to be assassinated by Arabs
and for our flesh to be eaten by Arabs
and to be disemboweled by Arabs
and for our graves to be opened by Arabs
How do we escape this destiny?
For, the Arabic dagger doesn't differentiate between
the necks of men
and the necks of women

Balqis,
They blew you up
In this land,
all funerals start in *Karbala*
and end in *Karbala*
I won't read history any longer
My fingers are on fire
and my clothes are covered in blood
Here we are, entering the Stone Age
Every day we go back one thousand years

In Beirut, the sea had retired
after the departure of your eyes
And poetry is asking
about its unfinished verses
and no one responds

Sorrow, O Balqis,
squeezes my heart as if it were an orange
Now, I know the dilemma of words
the deadlock of an impossible language

بلقيس
يا صفصافةً أرْخَت ضفائرها علي
ويا زرافة كبرياء
بلقيس
إن قضاءنا العربي أن يغتالنا عربٌ
ويأكل لحمنا عربٌ
ويبقر بطننا عربٌ
ويفتح قبرنا عربٌ
فكيف نفرُ من هذا القضاء؟
فالخنجر العربي.. ليس يُقيّم فرقاً
بين أعناق الرجال
وبين أعناق النساء

بلقيس
إن هم فجروك.. فعندنا
كل الجنائز تبتدي في كربلاء
وتنتهي في كربلاء
لن أقرأ التاريخ بعد اليوم
إن أصابعي اشتعلت
وأثوابي تغطيها الدماء
ها نحن ندخل عصرنا الحجري
نرجع كل يوم، ألف عام للوراء

البحر في بيروت
بعد رحيل عينيك استقال
والشعر.. يسأل عن قصيدته
التي لم تكتمل كلماتها
ولا أحدٌ.. يجيب على السؤال

الحزن يا بلقيس
يَعصُرُ مهجتي كالبرتقالة
الآن.. أعرف مأزق الكلمات
أعرف ورطة اللغة المحالة

And I—the one who invented letters—
don't know how to start a letter
The sword enters my flank
and that of the sentence
You are a civilization, Balqis, and a woman is a civilization

Balqis,
You are my great Gospel
Who stole my Gospel?
You are the writing before writing existed
You are the lighthouse and the island

Balqis,
O the moon that was buried in between stones
Now the curtain is pulled
the curtain is pulled
I am going to say during the interrogation
that I know the names and the things and the prisoners
and the martyrs and the poor and the oppressed
And I am going to say that I know the executioner who killed my wife
and the faces of all the investigators
And say that our chastity is adultery
and that our piety is dirtiness
And say that our struggle is a lie
and that there is no difference
between politics and prostitution
I will say that I know the murderers
and say
that our Arabic time specializes in slaughtering jasmines
and killing all the prophets
and all the missionaries
Even the green eyes are devoured by the Arabs
Even the rings and the fingers
and the bracelets and the mirrors and the toys
Even the stars are afraid of my homeland

وأنا الذي اخترع الرسائل
لست أدري.. كيف أبتدئ الرسالة
السيف يدخل لحم خاصرتي
وخاصرة العبارة
كل الحضارة، أنت يا بلقيس، والأنثى حضارة

بلقيس: أنت بشارتي الكبرى
فمَنْ سرق البشارة؟
أنت الكتابة قبلما كانت كتابة
أنت الجزيرة والمنارة

بلقيس
يا قمري الذي طمروه ما بين الحجارة
الآن ترتفع الستارة
الآن ترتفع الستارة
سأقول في التحقيق
إني أعرف الأسماء.. والأشياء.. والسجناء
والشهداء.. والفقراء.. والمستضعفين
وأقول إني أعرف السيّاف قاتل زوجتي
ووجوه كل المخبرين
وأقول: إن عفافنا عهرٌ
وتقوانا قذارة
وأقول: إن نضالنا كذبٌ
وأن لا فرق
ما بين السياسة والدعارة!!
سأقول في التحقيق
إني قد عرفت القاتلين
وأقول
إن زماننا العربي مختصٌّ بذبح الياسمين
وبقتل كل الأنبياء
وقتل كل المرسلين
حتى العيون الخضر
يأكلها العرب
حتى الضفائر.. والخواتم
والأساور.. والمرايا.. واللعب
حتى النجوم تخاف من وطني

and I don't know why
Even birds escape from my country
and I don't know why
Even the planets and the boats and the clouds
Even the notebooks and the books
and everything beautiful
all of it against Arabs
O Balqis, the precious pearl,
Is killing women an Arab hobby?
Or are we since the beginning
professional murderers?

Balqis,
my beautiful mare,
I am ashamed of my whole history
This is a country where mares are killed
This is a country where mares are killed
Since the day they killed you, Balqis,
O the most beautiful country,
one doesn't know how to live in this land
One does not know how to die in this land
I am still paying with my blood
the highest fine
but the sky had wanted me to be lonely
like the leaves of the trees
Are poets born from the womb of suffering?
Is the poem a stab in the heart without a cure?
Or is it only me
whose eyes summarize the history of crying?

ولا أدري السبب
حتى الطيور تفرُّ من وطني
ولا أدري السبب
حتى الكواكب.. والمراكب.. والسحب
حتى الدفاتر.. والكتب
وجميع أشياء الجمال
جميعها.. ضد العرب
لما تناثر جسمك الضوئي
يا بلقيس
يا لؤلؤةً كريمة
فكَّرْتُ: هل قَتْلُ النساء هوايةٌ عربيةٌ
أم أننا في الأصل، محترفو جريمة؟

بلقيس
يا فرسي الجميلة.. إنني
من كل تاريخي خجول
هذي بلادٌ يقتلون بها الخيول
هذي بلادٌ يقتلون بها الخيول
من يوم أن نَحَروك
يا بلقيس
يا أحلى وطن
لا يعرف الإنسان كيف يعيش في هذا الوطن
لا يعرف الإنسان كيف يموت في هذا الوطن
ما زلتُ أدفع من دمي
أعلى جزاء
كي أسعِد الدنيا.. ولكن السماء
شاءت بأن أبقى وحيداً
مثل أوراق الشتاء
هل يولدُ الشعراء من رحم الشقاء؟
وهل القصيدة طعنةٌ
في القلب.. ليس لها شفاء؟
أم أنني وحدي الذي
عيناه تختصران تاريخ البكاء؟

I will say during the interrogation
how my gazelle died by the sword of *Abou-Lahab*
All the thieves from the Gulf to the ocean
destroy and burn and steal and take bribes and rape women
as *Abou-Lahab* wishes
The dogs *Abou-Lahab* hires
eat and get drunk at his expense
No wheat may be grown on this earth
without the permission of *Abou-Lahab*
No child may be born here
unless the mother visits *Abou-Lahab's* bed
No prison opens without *Abou-Lahab's* permission
No beheading without his orders
I will say during the interrogation
how my princess was raped
how they divided the turquoise of her eyes
and her wedding ring
and tell how they divided her hair
that flows like golden rivers
I will say during the interrogation
how they stole the verses of her Quran
and set it on fire
I will tell how they drained her blood
and possessed her mouth
and did not leave roses in it or grapes
Is Balqis's death
the only victory
in the history of the Arabs?

سأقول في التحقيق
كيف غزالتي ماتت بسيف أبي لهب
كل اللصوص من الخليج إلى المحيط
يدمرون.. ويحرقون
وينهبون.. ويرتشون
ويعتدون على النساء
كما يريد أبو لهب
كل الكلاب موظفون
ويأكلون
ويسكرون
على حساب أبي لهب
لا قمحةٌ في الأرض
تنبت دون رأي أبي لهب
لا طفلٌ يولد عندنا
إلا وزارت أمه يوماً
فراش أبي لهب!!
لا سجنٌ يُفتَح
دون رأي أبي لهب
لا رأسٌ يُقطع
دون أمر أبي لهب
سأقول في التحقيق
كيف أميرتي اغتُصِبَت
وكيف تقاسموا فيروز عينيها
وخاتم عرسها
وأقول كيف تقاسموا الشعر الذي
يجري كأنهار الذهب
سأقول في التحقيق
كيف سطوا على آيات مصحفها الشريف
وأضرموا فيه اللهب
سأقول كيف استنزفوا دمها
وكيف استملكوا فمها
فما تركوا به ورداً.. ولا تركوا عِنب
هل موت بلقيس
هو النصر الوحيد
بكل تاريخ العرب؟؟

Balqis,
my lover,
How I'm drunk with your love!
The prophets are liars;
they squat
and ride on people
and they have no message
If they had brought us from sad Palestine
a star
or an orange
If they had carried to us
from the coast of Gaza
a small stone
or an oyster
If they—in a quarter-century—
had freed an olive
or returned a lemon
and erased the shame of history
I would have thanked your murderers
But they left Palestine alone
to kill a gazelle
What would poetry say about that, O Balqis?
In the time of populism
of cowardice,
the Arab world is crushed and oppressed
and its tongue is cut
We are the crime at its best
so what good are *Al-Aqd al Farid* and *Al-Aghani*?

بلقيس
يا معشوقتي حتى الثمالة
الأنبياء الكاذبون
يقرفصون
ويركبون على الشعوب
ولا رسالة
لو أنهم حملوا إلينا
من فلسطين الحزينة
نجمةً
أو برتقالة
لو أنهم حملوا إلينا
من شواطئ غزة
حجراً صغيراً
أو محارة
لو أنهم من ربع قرنٍ حرروا
زيتونةً
أو أرجعوا ليمونةً
ومحوا عن التاريخ عاره
لشكرْتُ من قتلوك.. يا بلقيس
يا معشوقتي حتى الثمالة
لكنهم تركوا فلسطيناً
ليغتالوا غزالة!!
ماذا يقول الشعر، يا بلقيس
في هذا الزمان؟
ماذا يقول الشعر؟
في العصر الشعوبي
المجوسي
الجبان
والعالم العربي
مسحوقٌ.. ومقموعٌ
ومقطوع اللسان
نحن الجريمة في تفوقها
فما (العقد الفريد) وما (الأغاني)؟؟

They took you, my love, from my hands
They took the poem from my mouth
They took writing and reading
and childhood and hope
Balqis, O Balqis,
O the tear that drops over the eyelashes of a violin,
I taught your killers the secrets of love
but before the end of the race,
they killed my mare

Balqis,
I ask your forgiveness. Maybe
your life was a sacrifice for mine
because whoever killed you meant to kill my verses
Sleep in God's grace, my beautiful
Poetry after you is impossible
and femininity is impossible
Generations of children
will ask about your long braids
Generations of lovers
will read about you, O the original teacher
And the Arabs will know one day
that they killed the Prophet
Killed the Prophet
K I L L E D
The Prophet

أخذوك أيتها الحبيبة من يدي
أخذوا القصيدة من فمي
أخذوا الكتابةّ.. والقراءة
والطفولة.. والأماني
بلقيس.. يا بلقيس
يا دمعاً يُنَقِّط فوق أهداب الكمان
علَّمْتُ من قتلوك أسرار الهوى
لكنهم.. قبل انتهاء الشوط
قد قتلوا حصاني

بلقيس
أسألك السماح، فربما
كانت حياتك فديّةٌ لحياتي
إني أعرف جيداً
أن الذين تورطوا في القتل، كان مرادهم
أن يقتلوا كلماتي!!!
نامي بحفظ الله.. أيتها الجميلة
فالشعر بعدك مستحيلٌ
والأنوثة مستحيلة
ستظل أجيالٌ من الأطفال
تسأل عن ضفائرك الطويلة
وتظل أجيالٌ من العشاق
تقرأ عنك.. أيتها المعلمة الأصيلة
وسيعرف الأعراب يوماً
أنهم قتلوا الرسولة
قتلوا الرسولة
ق .. ت .. ل .. و .. ا
ال .. ر .. س .. و .. ل .. ة

Nineveh: An ancient Assyrian city located currently on the outskirt of the modern Iraqi city of Mosul.

Al-Samawa'l Bin Adyia: An Arabian poet and a warrior who lived in the first half of the sixth century AD. He was known for his loyalty. Hence, the Arabic idiom (more loyal than than Al-Samawa'l).

Al-Muhalhil: Al-Muhalhil Adi Ibn Rabia is a poet and a warrior from the Arabian peninsula sixth century AD. He was the hero in the famous *Epic of Adi* that evolved around the death of his brother.

Sheba: A kingdom in South Arabia in the first millennium BC. It is the current day, Yemen. The Queen of Sheba (Balqis in Arabic) was first mentioned in the Hebrew Bible. She brought gifts and spices to King Solomon in Jerusalem.

A'azamiah: An upscale neighborhood in the Iraqi capital, Baghdad, where Balqis grew up. It goes back to the Abbasid time.

Al-Rusafa: A district in Baghdad on the east side of the Tigris.

Zeineb and Omar: Nizar Qabani's children with his second wife, Balqis.

Karbala: A city in Iraq where a famous battle took place in the sixth century AD. The Battle was between Hussein Ibn Ali's supporters (the Shiites) and the Umayyad Caliphate's supporters (the Sunnis), in which Imam Hussein was killed. The city is a holy place for the Shiite Muslims where the Shrine of Imam Hussein is located.

Abou-Lahab: He was Prophet Muhammad's half paternal uncle. He opposed him and his followers and was condemned for antagonizing Islam and its principles.

Al-Aqd al Farid and Al-Aghani: Two Arabic philosophy and literature books written in the tenth century AD.

Notes in the Book of Defeat

1

My friends, I mourn with you the old language
and the old books
I mourn our speech which
has a hole in it like a worn-out shoe
I mourn the lexicon of debauchery, rants, and curses
I mourn. I mourn
the thinking that led to defeat

2

Sour in our mouths are the poems
Sour are the women's braids
Sour are the nights and the curtains and the seats
Sour are all things before us

3

O my sad nation,
You turned me in a second
from a poet who writes about love and longing
into a poet who writes with a knife

4

Because what we feel is heavier than what our pages can hold,
we should be ashamed of our verses

5

We lost the war, and that is no wonder
because we entered it
with our Oriental talent for making speeches
with our bravado that never killed a fly
Because we entered it
with the logic of the drum and the *rebab*

هوامش على دفاتر النكسة

أنعي لكم، يا أصدقائي، اللغة القديمة
والكتب القديمة
أنعي لكم
كلامنا المثقوب، كالأحذية القديمة
ومفردات العهر، والهجاء، والشتيمة
أنعي لكم.. أنعي لكم
نهاية الفكر الذي قاد إلى الهزيمة

2

مالحةٌ في فمنا القصائد
مالحةٌ ضفائر النساء
والليل، والأستار، والمقاعد
مالحةٌ أمامنا الأشياء

3

يا وطني الحزين
حوَّلْتَني بلحظةٍ
من شاعرٍ يكتب الحب والحنين
لشاعرٍ يكتب بالسكين

4

لأن ما نُحِسُّه أكبر من أوراقنا
لا بد أن نخجل من أشعارنا

5

إذا خسرنا الحرب لا غرابة
لأننا ندخلها
بكل ما يملك الشرقي من مواهب الخطابة
بالعنتريات التي ما قَتَلَتْ ذبابة
لأننا ندخلها
بمنطق الطبلة والرباب

6

The secret of our tragedy
is that our cry is louder than our voice
and our swords are taller than we are

7

This is the summary of our case:
We wear the shell of civilization
but our souls are still medieval

8

With the flute and *ney*,
victory is unattainable

9

Our masochism won for us
fifty thousand new tents

10

Don't curse the sky if it abandons you
Don't curse the circumstance
God gives victory to whom he desires
But God is not a blacksmith;
he will not make you swords

11

It pains me to hear the morning news
to hear the barking

12

Our enemies did not cross our borders
they crept, like ants, out of our eyes

6

السرُ في مأساتنا
صراخنا أضخم من أصواتنا
وسيفنا أطول من قاماتنا

7

خلاصة القضية
تُوجَز في عبارة
لقد لبسنا قشرة الحضارة
والروح جاهلية

8

بالناي والمزمار
لا يحدث انتصار

9

كلَّفَنا ارتجالنا
خمسين ألف خيمةٍ جديدة

10

لا تلعنوا السماء
إذا تخلَّتْ عنكم
لا تلعنوا الظروف
فالله يُؤتي النصر من يشاء
وليس حدَّاداً لديكم.. يصنع السيوف

11

يوجعُني أن أسمع الأنباء في الصباح
يوجعني.. أن أسمع النباح

12

ما دَخَلَ اليهود من حدودنا
وإنما
تسربوا كالنمل.. من عيوننا

13

We have been in the caves
for five thousand years
Our beards are long
Our currency is unrecognizable
Our eyes are ports for flies
My friends,
try to break the doors;
try to cleanse your thoughts
to wash your clothes
My friends,
try to read a book
to write a book
to plant letters, pomegranates, or grapes
to sail to the lands of fog and snow
People outside the caves don't know who you are
People think of you as sort of wolves

14

Our skin is numb
Our souls are bankrupt
Our days circle around visitors and chess games
and drowsy hours in the sun
Are we *"The best nation given to people"*?

15

It was possible for the oil—plentiful in our desert—
to turn into a dagger of flame and fire
But—to the shame of the nobles from *Quraysh*,
to the shame of the free people from *Ous* and *Nizar*—
oil is poured under the feet of concubines

13

خمسة آلاف سنة
ونحن في السرداب
ذقوننا طويلةٌ
نقودنا مجهولةٌ
عيوننا مرافئ الذباب
يا أصدقائي:
جرّبوا أن تكسروا الأبواب
أن تغسلوا أفكاركم، وتغسلوا الأثواب
يا أصدقائي
جرّبوا أن تقرأوا كتاب
أن تكتبوا كتاب
أن تزرعوا الحروف، والرمان، والأعناب
أن تبحروا إلى بلاد الثلج والضباب
فالناس يجهلونكم.. في خارج السرداب
الناس يحسبونكم نوعاً من الذئاب

14

جلودنا ميّتة الإحساس
أرواحنا تشكو من الإفلاس
أيامنا تدور بين الزار، والشطرنج، والنعاس
هل نحن "خير أمةٍ قد أُخرجت للناس"؟

15

كان بوسْعِ نفطنا الدافق بالصحاري
أن يستحيل خنجراً
من لهبٍ ونار
لكنه
واخجلة الأشراف من قريشٍ
وخجلة الأحرار من أوسٍ ومن نزار
يُراق تحت أرجل الجواري

16

We run in the streets
we drag people with *ropes*
without thinking
We break windows and locks
We praise like frogs
We swear like frogs
We turn our dwarfs into giants
and our nobles into scoundrels
We improvise heroism
and sit in the mosques
lazy and unmotivated,
write verses and proverbs
and beg God to defeat our enemies

17

If someone grants me safety
If I could meet the Sultan
I would say,
"My Sultan,
Your vicious dogs tear my clothes
and your spies are always after me
Their eyes after me, their noses after me
their feet after me
Like inescapable fate, like judgment
they interrogate my wife
and take down my friend's names
Your majesty, my Sultan,
Because I approached your mute fences
because I uncovered my sorrow and despair
they beat me with their boots

16

نركض في الشوارع
نحمل تحت إبطنا الحبال
نمارس السحل بلا تبَصر
نحطِّم الزجاج والأقفال
نمدح كالضفادع
نشتم كالضفادع
نجعل من أقزامنا أبطال
نجعل من أشرافنا أنذالاً
نرتجل البطولة ارتجالًا
نقعد في الجوامع
تنابلاً.. كسالى
نَشطُر الأبيات، أو نؤلف الأمثال
ونشحذ النصر على عدونا
من عنده تعالى

17

لو أحدٌ يمنحني الأمان
لو كنت أستطيع أن أقابل السلطان
قلت له: يا سيدي السلطان
كلابك المفترسات مزَّقت ردائي
ومخبروك دائماً ورائي
عيونهم ورائي
أنوفهم ورائي
أقدامهم ورائي
كالقدر المحتوم، كالقضاء
يستجوبون زوجتي
ويكتبون عندهم
أسماء أصدقائي
يا حضرة السلطان
لأنني اقتربت من أسوارك الصماء
لأنني
حاولت أن أكشف عن حزني.. وعن بلائي
ضُرِبْت بالحذاء

and forced me to eat my shoes
Your majesty,
Your majesty, my Sultan,
We lost the war twice
because half of our citizens have no tongues
What use is a citizen without a tongue?
Because half of our citizens are besieged inside the walls
like ants or rats"
If someone grants my safety
from the Sultan's men
I would tell him,
"You lost the war twice
because you became separated from the human cause"

18

Had we not buried the *unity of Egypt and Syria* in the soil
had we not torn its pliant body with bayonets
had we kept it in the eyes and the eyelashes
dogs would not have savaged our flesh

19

We want an angry generation
We want a generation that can plow the horizons
and dig out history's roots to cultivate their minds
We want the new generation to be different:
relentless, unforgiving, uncompromising,
one that doesn't know hypocrisy
We need a generation—
a giant that can lead

أرغمني جندك أن آكل من حذائي
يا سيدي
يا سيدي السلطان
لقد خَسِرْتَ الحرب مرتين
لأن نصف شعبنا.. ليس له لسان
ما قيمة الشعب الذي ليس له لسان؟
لأن نصف شعبنا
محاصرٌ كالنمل والجرذان
في داخل الجدران
لو أحدٌ يمنحني الأمان
من عسكر السلطان
قلت له: لقد خَسِرْتَ الحرب مرتين
لأنك انفصلت عن قضية الإنسان

18

لو أننا لم نَدْفُن الوحدة في التراب
لو لم نمزّق جسمها الطري بالحراب
لو بَقَيَتْ في داخل العيون والأهداب
لما استباحت لحمّنا الكلاب

19

نريد جيلاً غاضباً
نريد جيلاً يفلح الآفاق
وينكش التاريخ من جذوره
وينكش الفكر من الأعماق
نريد جيلاً قادماً
مختلف الملامح
لا يغفر الأخطاء.. لا يسامح
لا ينحني
لا يعرف النفاق
نريد جيلاً
رائداً
عملاق

20

You children, from the ocean to the gulf,
you are the wheat stalks of hope
You are the generation that will break the chains
and vanish the illusion
and the opium in our heads
You children,
you are still innocent and pure
like the morning dew, like snow
Don't read about our defeated generation;
we are losers
and worthless as the rind of a watermelon
We are gnawed, gnawed like the insoles of our shoes
Don't read our news
Don't trace our tracks
Don't accept our ideas
We are the generation of vomit and syphilis and cough
We are the generation of quackery and trickery
You children are the spring's rain
and the wheat stalks of hope
You are the seed of fertility in our barren lives
You are the generation that will defeat the defeat.

This poem was a turning point in Nizar's poetry. After he wrote it, he was banned from entering Egypt. Arabic radios and televisions blocked any song that included his lyrics for a while. After the Six-Day War with Israel (June 5-10, 1967), Nizar's poetry became more political and targeted the dictatorial regimes in the Arab world. The Six-Day War took place between Israel and Syria, Egypt, and Jordan. Israel won the war and captured the Gaza Strip from Palestine, the Sinai Peninsula from Egypt, the West Bank from Jordan, and the Golan Heights from Syria.

20

يا أيها الأطفال
من المحيط للخليج، أنتم سنابل الآمال
وأنتم الجيل الذي سيكسر الأغلال
ويقتل الأفيون في رؤوسنا
ويقتل الخيال
يا أيها الأطفال أنتم – بعدُ– طيبون
وطاهرون، كالندى والثلج، طاهرون
لا تقرأوا عن جيلنا المهزوم يا أطفال
فنحن خائبون
ونحن، مثل قشرة البطيخ، تافهون
ونحن منخورون.. منخورون.. كالنعال
لا تقرأوا أخبار
لا تقتفوا آثارنا
لا تقبلوا أفكارنا
فنحن جيل القيء، والزهري، والسعال
ونحن جيل الدَّجَل، والرقص على الحبال
يا أيها الأطفال:
يا مطر الربيع.. يا سنابل الآمال
أنتم بذور الخصب في حياتنا العقيمة
وأنتم الجيل الذي سيهزم الهزيمة

Rebab: A string musical instrument used in the Middle East and North Africa during the eighth century AD.

Ney—also known as reed pipe: This is the oldest wind musical instrument that is still in use. It has been around for over 5,000 years and is still primarily used in Arabic music.

Fifty thousand tents: It refers to the Palestinians who were displaced after the Six-Day War and lived in tents in neighboring countries.

"The best nation given to people": A verse in the Quran, interpreted by some as indicating that Islam is the best nation that exists.

Quraysh: An Arab tribe that lived in Mecca. The Prophet Mouhamad was born to this tribe.

Ous: Is a pre-Islamic tribe that joined Islam when the Prophet Muhammad visited Madinah.

Nizar. Nizar Bin Maed: He was the eighteenth grandfather of the Prophet Muhammad.

Dragging with ropes: A known torture practice in the Arab world, where the body is pulled with a rope on the ground, either by hands or attached to a moving vehicle.

Syria and Egypt's unity: Syria and Egypt were united as a sovereign state in 1958, with Cairo as the capital, known as the United Arab Republic. Syria seceded in 1961. It is commonly believed that if the two countries had remained united, they might have won the Six-Day War.

I Read Your Body, and I Educate Myself

1

When the dialogue between your bathing breasts
and the tribes fighting over the water stopped,
the age of decay started.
The cloud boycotted the rain for five hundred years
and birds announced a strike and quit flying
Wheat stalks became barren
and the moon took the shape of an oil bottle

2

The day they expelled me from the tribe
because I left a poem and a rose outside your tent's door,
the age of decay started
The age of decay is not the ignorance of the grammar principles;
it is the ignorance of the feminism principles
it is erasing all women's names
from the memories of the land

3

Oh my love
What kind of nation is this
that deals with love like traffic police?
It considers a rose a conspiracy against the regime
and a poem a secret post against it
What kind of a nation is this
drawn in the shape of a yellow grasshopper;
it crawls on its abdomen from the ocean to the gulf
from the gulf to the ocean
speaks like a saint during the day
and swoons over a woman's naval at night

أقرأ جسدَكِ.. وأتثقَّف

1
يوم توقَّف الحوار بين نهديك المغتسلين بالماء
وبين القبائل المتقاتلة على الماء،
بَدأتْ عصور الانحطاط
أعلَنتْ الغيوم الإضراب عن المطر
لمدة خمسمئة سنة
وأعلَنتْ العصافير الإضراب عن الطيران
وامتَنَعَتْ السنابل عن إنجاب الأولاد
وصار شكل القمر كشكل زجاجة النفط

2
يوم طردوني من القبيلة
لأني تركت قصيدةً على باب خيمتك
وتركتُ لك معها وردة
بدأت عصور الانحطاط
إن عصور الانحطاط ليست الجهل بمبادئ النحو
والصَرْف
لكنها الجهل بمبادئ الأنوثة
وشطب أسماء جميع النساء من ذاكرة الوطن

3
آه يا حبيبتي
ما هو هذا الوطن الذي يتعامل مع الحب
كشرطيْ سير؟
فيَعتبر الوردة مؤامرةً على النظام
ويَعتبر القصيدة منشوراً سرياً ضده
ما هو هذا الوطن المرسوم على شكل جرادة صفراء
تزحف على بطنها من المحيط إلى الخليج
من الخليج إلى المحيط
والذي يتكلم في النهار كقديس
ويدوخ في الليل على سرة امرأة

4
What kind of a nation is this
that removes love from the curriculum
and deletes the eyes of women from a poem?
What kind of nation is this
that battles each rain cloud
that opens a secret file for every breast
and interrogates each flower?

5

Oh, my love,
What do we do with this nation
that is afraid of the woman's body
afraid of desiring it
fearful that a woman's voice on the phone may ruin
the purity of ablution?
What do we do with this nation
that knows everything about the October Revolution
and the African American uprising
and the revolution of *Al-Karameta*
and deals with women as if it were *Tariqa* sheik?
What do we do with this nation
that is lost between the writing of the imams
and the writing of Lenin
between debating articles and pornography
between books of theology and Playboy magazines
between the *Moutazella* band and the Beatles
between *Rabeaa Al-Adouieh* and *Emanuel*?

O love,
You are amazing like children's toys
I am civilized because I love you
My poems are historical because they are written during your
   lifetime

4
ما هو هذا الوطن؟
الذي ألغى مادة الحب من مناهجه المدرسية
وألغى فنَّ الشعر
وعيون النساء
ما هو هذا الوطن؟
الذي يمارس العدوان على كل غمامةٍ ماطرة
ويفتح لكل نهدٍ ملفاً سرياً
ويُنظِّم مع كل وردةٍ محضر تحقيق!!

5
يا حبيبتي
ماذا نفعل في هذا الوطن؟
الذي يخاف أن يرى جسده في المرآة
حتى لا يشتهيه
ويخاف أن يسمع صوت امرأةٍ في التلفون
حتى لا ينقض وضونه
ماذا نفعل في هذا الوطن؟
الذي يعرف كل شيءٍ عن ثورة أكتوبر
وثورة الزنج
وثورة القرامطة
ويتصرف مع النساء كأنه شيخ طريقه
ماذا نفعل في هذا الوطن الضائع
بين مؤلفات الإمام الشافعي.. ووفيات لينين
بين المادية الجدلية.. وصور (البورنو)
بين كتب التفسير.. ومجلة (البلاي بوي)
بين فرقة (المعتزلة).. وفرقة (البيتلز)
بين رابعة العدوية.. وبين (إيمانويل)

أيتها المدهشة كألعاب الأطفال
إنني أعتبر نفسي متحضراً
لأني أحبك
وأعتبر قصائدي تاريخيةً.. لأنها عاصرتك

Time was a possibility before your eyes
and Time after them is a shrapnel
Don't ask me why I am with you
I want to exit my backwardness and enter the time of water
I want to escape the republic of thirst
and enter the republic of Magnolia
I want to exit my tribalism
sit under the trees
bathe in the springs
and learn the names of flowers
I want you to teach me reading and writing
To write on your body is the beginning of knowledge
to enter it is to enter civilization
Your body is not against education
it is the education
He who doesn't read the notebook of your body
is illiterate

Al-Karameta: A branch of Ismaili Shia Islam; they established a religious republic in the ninth century AD.
Tariqa: A School of Sufism that teaches the seeking of "the ultimate truth."
Moutazela: A group of religious debaters in the Umayyad Caliphate.
Rabeaa Al-Adouieh: An Iraqi woman renowned as a poet and singer in the eighth century AD. She was a devout Sufi; her extreme piety led her to renounce the role of women in pre-Muslim society. *Emanuel* is a Hebrew name given to Jesus, meaning "God with us." Qabbani uses both names as exemplars of lives presumably abstinent from sex.

كل زمن قبل عينيك هو احتمال
وكل زمن بعدهما هو شظايا
ولا تسأليني لماذا أنا معك
إنني أريد أن أخرج من تخلُّفي
وأدخل في زمن الماء
أريد أن أهرب من جمهورية العطش
وأدخل جمهورية المانوليا
أريد أن أخرج من بداوتي
وأجلس تحت الشجر
وأغتسل بماء الينابيع
وأتعلم أسماء الزهار
أريد أن تعلميني القراءة والكتابة
فالكتابة على جسدك أول المعرفة
والدخول إليه دخول إلى الحضارة
إن جسدك ليس ضد الثقافة
لكنه الثقافة
من لا يقرأ دفاتر جسدك
يبقى طول حياته.. أمياً

Citizens Without a Nation

Citizens without a nation
chased on the maps of time like birds
Travelers without papers and dead without coffins
We are the prostitutes of the time
Every leader sells us and collect the price
We are the slave-women
they send us from room to room
from hand to hand
from one idol to another
We run like dogs every night
from Aden to Tangier
We look for a tribe to accept us
We look for a curtain to cover us
We look for a home

Our children are around us
their backs are hunched down into the old dictionaries
We are citizens in the cities of cries
Our coffee is made from the blood of *Karbala*
Our wheat is kneaded with the flesh of *Karbala*
Our food and drink
our flag and tradition
our flowers and graves
our skin is sealed with the seal of *Karbala*
No one knows us in this desert
neither a camel nor a palm tree
neither a peg nor a stone
nor *Hind* nor *Afraa* knows us
Our documents are suspicious
Our thoughts are strange

مواطنون دونما وطن

مواطنون دونما وطن
مطاردون كالعصافير على خرائط الزمن
مسافرون دون أوراق.. وموتى دونما كفن
نحن بغايا العصر
كل حاكم يبيعنا ويقبض الثمن
نحن جواري القصر
يرسلوننا من حجرة لحجرة
من قبضة لقبضة
من مالك لمالك
ومن وثن إلى وثن
نركض كالكلاب كل ليلة
من عدنٍ لطنجة
نبحث عن قبيلة تقبلنا
نبحث عن ستارة تسترنا
وعن سكن

وحولنا أولادنا
احدودبت ظهورهم في المعاجم القديمة
مواطنون نحن في مدائن البكاء
قهوتنا مصنوعة من دم كربلاء
حنطتنا معجونة بلحم كربلاء
طعامنا.. شرابنا
عاداتنا.. راياتنا
زهورنا.. قبورنا
جلودنا مختومة بختم كربلاء
لا أحد يعرفنا في هذه الصحراء
لا نخلة.. ولا ناقة
لا وتد.. ولا حجر
لا هند.. لا عفراء
أوراقنا مريبة
أفكارنا غريبة

Our names don't look like names
Neither those who lap up our petroleum know us
nor those who drink suffering and tears

We are arrested inside our rulers' narrative
inside the religion as our Imams interpret it
We are arrested inside the sorrow, and sorrow is what is most
   beautiful about us
We are watched in the cafés
in our houses
in the womb of our mothers
Everywhere we turn, we find the Secret Service waiting for us
drinking our coffee
sleeping in our beds
messing with our mail
looking through our papers
entering our noses
and exiting with our coughs
Our tongue is cut
Our head is severed
Our bread is soaked with fear and tears
If we complain to our protector,
we're told: forbidden
If we plead to God,
we're told: forbidden
And if we call for the prophet to help us,
we are handed a one-way visa
And if we ask for a pencil to write the last poem
or our last will,
they change the subject

O my nation, crucified on the walls of hatred
O the ball of fire rolling towards the abyss,
No one from *Madar* or *Thaqif*

أسماؤنا لا تشبه الأسماء
فلا الذين يشربون النفط يعرفوننا
ولا الذين يشربون الدمع والشقاء

معتقلون داخل النصّ الذي يكتبه حكامنا
معتقلون داخل الدين كما فسره إمامُنا
معتقلون داخل الحزن.. وأحلى ما بنا أحزاننا
مراقبون نحن في المقهى
وفي البيت
وفي أرحام أمهاتنا
حيث تلفتنا وجدنا المخبر السري في انتظارنا
يشرب من قهوتنا
ينام في فراشنا
يعبث في بريدنا
ينكش في أوراقنا
يدخل في أنوفنا
يخرج من سعالنا
لساننا.. مقطوع
ورأسنا.. مقطوع
وخبزنا مبلل بالخوف والدموع
إذا تظلّمنا إلى حامي الحمى
قيل لنا: ممنـــــوع
وإذا تضرَّعنا إلى رب السماء
قيل لنا: ممنـــــوع
وإن هتفنا.. يا رسول الله كن في عوننا
يعطوننا تأشيرة من غير ما رجوع
وإن طلبنا قلماً لنكتب القصيدة الأخيرة
أو نكتب الوصية الأخيرة
قبيل أن نموت شنقاً
غيِّروا الموضوع

يا وطني المصلوب فوق حائط الكراهية
يا كرة النار التي تسير نحو الهاوية
لا أحد من مضَرْ.. أومن بني ثقيف

gave this bleeding nation
a unit of transfusion
No one on the stretch of this patched *abaya*
gave it a coat or a hat
O my nation, broken like autumn's leaves,
We are uprooted from our place like trees
migrants from our hopes and memories
Our eyes are afraid of our voice
Our rulers are gods; blue blood runs in their veins
and we are descendants of slaves
Neither the nobles of *Al-Hijaz* know us, nor the desert's mob
Neither *Abu Al-Tayyib* hosts us, nor *Abu Al-Atahiya*
If one tyrant leaves
we submit to another

We are immigrants from the ports of exhaustion
No one wants us
from the sea in Beirut to the Arabian Sea
neither the Fatimid nor the *Karameta*
neither the *Mamluks* nor the *Barmakids*
neither the devils nor the angels
No one wants us
No one reads us
In the cities of salt that slaughter millions of books a year
where the government's investigators are the Godfathers of literature,
no one reads us
We are travelers in the boat of political parties
Our leader is a mercenary
and our Sheik is a pirate
We are stuffed into cages like rats
No port will accept us
No bar will accept us
No woman will accept us

أعطى لهذا الوطن الغارق بالنزيف
زجاجة من دمه
أو بوله الشريف
لا أحد على امتداد هذه العباءة المرقعة
أهداك يوماً معطفاً أو قبعة
يا وطني المكسور مثل عشبة الخريف
مُقتَلعون نحن كالأشجار من مكاننا
مُهَجرون من أمانينا وذكرياتنا
عيوننا تخاف من أصواتنا
حكامنا آلهة يجري الدم الأزرق في عروقهم
ونحن نسلُ الجارية
لا سادة الحجاز يعرفوننا.. ولا رعاع البادية
ولا أبو الطيب يستضيفنا.. ولا أبو العتاهية
إذا مضى طاغية
سلّمنا لطاغية

مهاجرون نحن من مرافئ التعب
لا أحد يريدنا
من بحر بيروت إلى بحر العرب
لا الفاطميون.. ولا القرامطة
ولا المماليك... ولا البرامكة
ولا الشياطين.. ولا الملائكة
لا أحد يريدنا
لا أحد يقرؤنا
في مدن الملح التي تَذبَح في العام ملايين الكتب
لا أحد يقرؤنا
في مدنٍ صارت بها مباحث الدولة عرّاب الأدب
مسافرون نحن في سفينة الأحزاب
قائدنا مرتزق
وشيخنا قرصان
مكومون داخل الأقفاص كالجرذان
لا مرفأ يقبلنا
لا حانة تقبلنا
لا امرأة تقبلنا

The passports we carry are issued by the Devil
Everything we write
is rejected by the Sultan

Travelers outside of place and time
lost our money and luggage
lost our children
lost our names
lost our identity
lost our safety
Neither the *Hashemites* nor the *Qahtan* know us
Neither the *Rabiaas* nor the *Shybans*
nor do the people of Lenin or Reagan know us

O my nation,
All birds have a home
except for the seekers of freedom:
they die outside their homelands

كل الجوازات التي نحملها
أصدرها الشيطان
كل الكتابات التي نكتبها
لا تعجب السلطان

مسافرون خارج الزمان والمكان
مسافرون ضيعوا نقودهم.. وضيعوا متاعهم
ضيعوا أبناءهم
وضيعوا أسماءهم
وضيعوا انتماءهم
وضيعوا الإحساس بالأمان
فلا بنو هاشم يعرفوننا.. ولا بنو قحطان
ولا بنو ربيعة.. ولا بنو شيبان
ولا بنو "لينين" يعرفوننا
ولا بنو ريغان

يا وطني.. كـل العصافير لها منـازل
إلا العصافير التي تحترف الحريّة
فهي تمـوت خارج الأوطـان

In 1985, Nizar read this poem at the Merbid Festival of Poetry in Baghdad. It is said that Nizar was allowed to finish reading on the podium only to honor "literary immunity." After he left the stage, he was advised to leave the country as soon as possible to save his neck, which he did. He was not allowed to enter Iraq for a while after that. The poem was banned from publication in many Arab countries.

Karbala: A city in Iraq where a famous battle took place in the sixth century AD. The Battle was between Hussein Ibn Ali's supporters, (the Shiites) and the Umayyad Caliphate's supporters, in which Imam Hussein was killed. The city is a holy place for the Shiite Muslims where the Shrine of Imam Hussein is located.

Hind: Hind Bint Utbah: An Arab poet of the seventh century AD. She was the wife of Abu Sufyan, a powerful man in Mecca. She was known for her courage and wisdom.

Afraa: Afraa Bint Mouhaser: An Arab poet in the seventh century AD. She was denied marrying the man she loved and was forced to marry another. She remained faithful to her lover even after he died, it is said, of a broken heart.

Madar: He was the seventeenth grandfather of the Prophet Muhammad. He was the first to make camel shoes.

Thaqif: This was a pre-Islamic tribe from Ta'if (in Saudi Arabia now). They worshiped the Arabian Goddess, Allat.

Abaya: A Middle Eastern cloak.

Al-Hijaz: A region in the west of Saudi Arabia, bordered by the Red Sea and Jordan.

Abu-Al-Tayyib: Al-Mutannabi: He was a poet from Iraq. He was considered one of the most prominent Arab poets of the tenth century AD. His poetry was the most influential in Arabic literature and is still taught in schools. His work was also translated into many languages.

Abu Al-Atahiya: An Iraqi poet of the eighth century AD, famous for being imprisoned for writing love poems to one of the Abbasid Caliph Al-Mahdi's concubines.

Fatimid Caliphate: A Shiite Caliphate. It originated in North Africa in the tenth Century AD and expanded across the Mediterranean coast, including Lebanon, Syria, and Tunisia. It made Egypt its center.

Al-Karameta: A branch of Ismaili Shia Islam; they established a religious republic in the ninth century AD.

Mamluk: Mamluk Sultanate. A thirteenth-century AD sultanate. It spanned Egypt and Al-Hijaz and lasted until the Ottoman conquest of Egypt in 1517.

Barmakids: An Iranian Dynasty from Balkh. They were known for their hospitality. They were originally Buddhist but assumed great political power under the Abbasid Caliphate. Ultimately, in the ninth century AD, their influence was feared, and they lost their favor, and many of their members were imprisoned or killed by the Calipha, Haroun Al-Rashid.

Hashemites: The kingdom of Iraq, founded in 1921 after the defeat of the Ottoman Empire, was ruled by the Hashemite rulers. Iraq was then called The Mamlekah Al-Iraqiah Al-Hashemiah.

Qahtan: A seventh-century AD Arab tribe based in Yemen.

Rabiaa: An Arab tribe that originated from Western Arabia and migrated to the Northeast, modern-day Bahrain.

Shyban: An Arab tribe that was based in Al-Jazira and expanded to Iraq and the Persian Gulf. The tribe is known for its quality poets.

Biographies

Nizar Qabbani (Syria, 1923-1998)

Nizar Qabbani was a diplomat, poet, and publisher whose work approached the sensitive subjects of eroticism, feminism, Arab nationalism, love, and religion. Much of his poetry speaks of the imprisonment that Arab society imposes on its women. Many of his political poems about Syria liken the country's colonization by France to the situation of Arab women.

He started writing poetry at the age of 16, and throughout over a half-century, Qabbani wrote 34 books of poetry. His poetry was published not only in books but in the newspapers and is heard in the lyrics of popular songs

Qabbani's first poetry book was published while studying law at Damascus University. The book shocked the Syrian conservative society with its open and provocative descriptions of women's bodies and with its sensual verses.

Qabbani graduated in 1945 with a degree in law and went to work for the Syrian Foreign Ministry. He continued to work at the Ministry until his resignation in 1966. During his time with the Foreign Ministry, he served posts in Cairo, Beirut, Istanbul, Madrid, London, and China.

Mr. Qabbani's second wife, Balqis, was killed in a bomb attack on the Iraqi embassy in Beirut in 1982. He expressed grief over her death in one of his most loved and famous poems, *Balqis*.

Qabbani opened his own publishing house in London in the early 1960s, and it rapidly became a powerful voice of lament for Arab causes.

When he died in 1998 at 75, the New York Times obituary was headlined "Nizar Qabbani, Sensual Arab Poet, Dies at 75." It quoted the Syrian poet Youssef Karkoutly, who said of Qabbani, "His poetry was as necessary to our lives as air."

RANA BITAR, WWW.RANABITAR.COM

Rana Bitar is a Syrian-American physician, poet, and writer. She holds a master's degree in English and Creative Writing from Southern New Hampshire University.

Her memoir, *The Long Tale of Tears and Smiles*, was published by Global Collective Publishers in August 2021.

She is the author of two poetry chapbooks, *A Loaf of Bread* (Unsolicited Press, 2019) and *Hold Your Breath* (Unsolicited Press, 2023).

A Loaf of Bread was a finalist in the "Concrete Wolf Chapbook Competition" in 2017 and won an honorable mention in "The 2017 Louis Award" for poetry.

Hold Your Breath was selected by The National Women's History Museum to be on Exhibit for their Coronavirus Journaling Project, and was featured in *The New York Times* on April 22, 2022.

Her poetry has appeared in many journals, including, *The Deadly Writers Patrol, DoveTales, Pittsburgh Poetry Review, Magnolia Review, El Portal, Pacific REVIEW, Black Coffee Review, The Phoenix, The Dewdrop, The International Human Rights Art Festival, The Charleston Anvil, Beltway Poetry Quarterly, The Sextant Review,*

Concrete Desert Review, *The Nonconformist Magazine*, *Seeing Things: Anthology of Poetry*, and *The New York Times*.

Her translation of Arabic poetry appeared in *The American Journal of Poetry*, *The Nonconformist*, *Illuminations*, *Beltway Poetry Quarterly*, and *AGNI*.

Her essays have been published in *The Pharos Journal*, *Med Page*, and *Pink Panther Magazine*.

Robert Bensen, https://robertbensen.com

Robert Bensen has published seven collections of his poetry, most recently *What Lightning Spoke* (Bright Hill Press), *Before* (Five Oaks Press), and *Orenoque, Wetumka & Other Poems* (Bright Hill Press). Poems have appeared in *Agni*, *Akwe:kon*, *Antioch Review*, *Callaloo*, *Caribbean Writer*, *Jamaica Journal*, *Native Realities*, *Paris Review*, *Partisan Review*, *Poetry Wales*, *Journal of Commonwealth Literature*, *Thomas Hardy Review*, and many others. He has also published essays and editions of West Indian and Native American writing. He directed the writing programs at Hartwick College, Oneonta, New York, from 1978 to 2017. His writing has won fellowships and awards from the National Endowment for the Arts, the National Endowment for the Humanities, Harvard University, the State of New York, Illinois Arts Council, the Robert Penn Warren Award, and others.

Acknowledgments

We would also like to acknowledge Mr. Muhamed Alkhalil (University of Arizona), whose Dissertation, *Nizar Qabbani: From Romance to Exile*, provided a wealth of information and guided us in placing the writing within its historical context.
    https://docplayer.net/88099907-Nizar-qabbani-from-romance-to-exile.html

Published poems:

The Nonconformist, March 18, March 25, 2021
"Standing in Lines" and "The Trains of Sorrows"

The Nonconformist, March 1, 2022
"A Lesson in Drawing"

The American Journal of Poetry, July 1, 2021
"I Love You to Life up the Sky" and "The Book of Love"

Illuminations, July 1, 2021
"I Love You and the Rest to Come" and "Citizens Without a Nation"

AGNI, Fall 2021
"Bread, Hashish, and the Moon"

Beltway Poetry Quarterly, Spring 2022
"African Breasts"

What Lightning Spoke, by Robert Bensen, Bright Hill Press, Inc., 2022
"African Breasts," "Bread, Hashish, and the Moon," and "A Lesson in Drawing"

www.ingramcontent.com/pod-product-compliance
Lightning Source LLC
Chambersburg PA
CBHW010051200426
43193CB00059B/2921